MW01105604

zen and tao
a little book of
buddhist thought
and meditation

dennis waller

edited by sherry thoman

Copyright © 2013 Dennis Waller

All rights reserved.

ISBN: 1482375451
ISBN-13: 978-1482375459

DEDICATION

This book is dedicated
to
Phil Walthall

"love ya brother"

CONTENTS

PREFACE

"Zen and Tao - A Little Book of Buddhist Thought and Meditation" is a collection of selected writings and translations of the Tao Te Ching, The Tree of Wisdom, and the Zen poem, Hsin Hsin Ming by Dennis Waller from his works on Zen and Taoist Thought. In addition to his works are included 50 Quotes from Chuang Tzu, Okakura Kakuzo, and Gautama Buddha.

This body of work offers the reader the opportunity to have an introduction to the various schools of Buddhist thought in one book. The purpose is to give the reader insights of the different perspectives from the Masters of Zen and the Tao Te Ching. Happy Reading

CHAPTER ONE- 50 QUOTES

Chuang Tzu - (389-286BC) An early interpreter of Taoism

1- You'll always find an answer within the sound of water.

2- I dreamed I was a butterfly, flitting around the sky, then I awoke. Now I am wondering, am I a man who dreamt of being a butterfly, or am I a butterfly dreaming that I am a man?

3- Happiness is in the absence of the striving for happiness.

4- If water derives lucidity from stillness, how much more the faculties of the mind! The mind of the Sage, being in repose, becomes the mirror of the universe, the speculum of all creation.

5- Those who realize their follies are not true fools.

6- I know the joy of the fishes through my own joy as I go walking along the same river.

7- We cling to our point of view as though everything depended on it. Yet, our opinions have no permanence; like autumn and winter, they gradually pass away.

8- Flow with whatever may happen and let your mind be free. Stay centered by accepting whatever you are doing. This is the ultimate state.

9- Great Wisdom is generous; petty wisdom is contentious

10- Men honor what lies within the sphere of knowledge, but do not realize how dependent they are on what lies beyond it.

11- All existing things are really one. We regard those that are beautiful and rare as valuable, and those that are ugly as foul and rotten. The foul and rotten may come to be transformed into what is rare and valuable, and the rare and valuable into what.

12- Those who seek to satisfy the mind of man by hampering it with ceremonies and music and affecting charity and devotion have lost their original nature.

13- The purpose of words is to convey ideas. When ideas are grasped, the words are forgotten. Where can I find a man who has forgotten the words?

14- Cherish that which is within you, and shut off that which is without, for too much knowledge is a curse.

15- Rewards and punishment is the lowest form of education.

16- Life comes from the Earth and life returns to the Earth.

17- There is nothing under the canopy of heaven greater than the tip of birds down in autumn, while the T'ai Mountain is small. Neither is there any longer life than that of a child cut off in infancy, while P'eng Tsu himself died young. The universe and I came into being together, I and everything therein are One.

Okakura Kakuzo (1862-1913) Author of "The Book of Tea"

1- The art of life lies in a constant readjustment to our surroundings.

2- Those who cannot feel the littleness of great things in themselves, are apt to overlook the greatness of little things in others.

3- For life is an expression, our unconscious actions the constant betrayal of our innermost thought. Perhaps we reveal ourselves too much in small things because we have so little of the great to conceal. The tiny incidents of daily routine are as much a commentary of racial ideas as the highest height of philosophy or poetry.

4- We take refuge in pride because we are afraid to tell the truth to ourselves.

5- Our mind is the canvas on which artist lay their color, their pigments are our emotions; their chiaroscuro the light of joy, the shadow of sadness. The masterpiece is ourselves, as we are of the masterpiece.

6- True beauty could be discovered only by one who mentally complete the incomplete.

7- We must know the whole play in order to properly act our parts; the conception of totality must never be lost in that of the individual.

8- We are ever brutal to those who love and serve us in silence, but the time may come when, for our cruelty, we shall be deserted by these best friends of ours.

9- People are not taught to be really virtuous, but to behave properly.

10- Those of us who know not the secret of properly regulating our own existence on this tumultuous sea of foolish troubles we call life are constantly in a state of misery while vainly trying to appear happy and contented. We stagger in the attempt to keep our moral equilibrium and see forerunners of the tempest in every cloud that floats on the horizon. Yet, there is joy and beauty in the roll of the billows as they sweep outward towards eternity. Why not enter into their spirit, or, like Lao Tzu, ride upon the hurricane itself?

11- But when we consider how small after all the cup of human enjoyment is, how soon overflowed with tears, how easily drained to the dregs in our quenchless thirst for infinity, we shall not blame ourselves for making so much of the tea-cup

12- Our standards of morality are begotten of the past needs to society, but is society to remain always the same?

13- In joy or sadness flowers are our constant friends.

Gautama Buddha

1- Do not dwell in the past, do not dream of the future, concentrate the mind on the present moment.

2- Health is the greatest gift, contentment the greatest wealth, faithfulness the best relationship.

3- We are shaped by our thoughts; we become what we think. When the mind is pure, joy follows like a shadow that never leaves.

4- Holding on to anger is like grasping a hot coal with the intent of throwing it at someone else; you are the one who gets burned.

5- To enjoy good health, to bring true happiness to one's family, to bring peace to all, one must first discipline and control one's own mind. If a man can control his mind he can find the way to enlightenment, and all wisdom and virtue will naturally come to him.

6- An insincere and evil friend is more to be feared than a wild beast; a wild beast may wound your body, but an evil friend will wound your mind.

7- The tongue is like a sharp knife, kills without drawing blood.

8- You can search throughout the entire universe for someone who is more deserving of your love and affection than you are yourself, and that person is not to be found anywhere. You yourself, as much as anybody in the entire universe deserves your love and affection.

9- Thousands of candles can be lighted from a single candle, and the life of the candle will not be shortened. Happiness never decreases by being shared.

10- However many holy words you read, however many you speak, what good will they do you if you do not act upon them?

11- Three things cannot be hidden long, the sun, the moon, and the truth.

12- It is better to conquer yourself than to win a thousand battles. Then the victory is yours. It cannot be taken from you, not by angels or by demons, not heaven or hell.

13- In the sky, there is no distinction of east and west; people create distinctions out of their own minds and they believe then to be true.

14- Do not overrate what you received, nor envy others. He who envies others does not obtain peace of mind.

15- To be idle is a short road to death and to be diligent is a way to life; foolish people are idle, wise people are diligent.

16- There is nothing more dreadful than the habit of doubt. Doubt separates people. It is poison that disintegrates friendships and breaks up pleasant relations. It is a thorn that irritates and hurts; it is a sword that kills.

17- The whole secret of existence is to have no fear. Never fear what will become of you, depend on no one. Only in the moment you reject all help are you freed.

18- To keep the body in good health is a duty, otherwise we shall not be able to keep our mind strong and clear.

19- Just as a candle cannot burn without fire, men cannot live without a spiritual life.

20- There are only two mistakes one can make along the road to truth; not going all the way and not starting.

CHAPTER TWO- HSIN HSIN MING

A Translation by Dennis Waller

The Great Way is not difficult for those who are indifferent and non-judgmental. Let go of attachment and desire and the Way reveals itself.

Make the slightest judgment and you are as far from the Way as Heaven is to Earth. If you want to experience the truth, then hold no judgments for or against anything.

Attraction and Aversion are afflictions of the mind. When the essence of the Way is not understood, the essential peace of the mind is fleeting.

The Great Way is as vast as the infinite universe. It is perfect and complete. It is your attraction and aversion that blinds you from the Way.

Do not try to catch or hold on to things. Do not be consumed by the abyss. Be still and know the oneness and the illusion fades away.

In striving to attain the tranquility of the Way, the mere

act of striving negates your quest. As long as you exist in the illusion of duality you'll never know the Way.

Those who don't live in the Great Way will continue to ebb and flow in the conflict of life. In denying the reality you miss the deeper meaning of reality. In defending the reality you miss the emptiness of reality.

The more your thoughts dwell on it, the further you will be. Still your thoughts and quiet your mind. In the silence of the Way, nothing is withheld from you.

To return to the source is to find meaning. To chase external desire and perversions is to miss the meaning. At the moment of enlightenment, you are beyond external desires and perversions.

Changes that seem to happen in the world are only outward perspectives based on attachment. Search not for the truth in this outward world. Become detached from judgment.

Do not cling to the views of duality. Be careful to avoid the traps of the external world. In choosing one or the other, right or wrong, the mind becomes entangled in dualism.

All dualities are born of the Oneness. Do not cling to any of them, not even this one. When the mind resides in the Oneness there is not one or the other, no right or wrong.

When things are no longer one or the other, right or wrong, they cease to exist. When the mind is no longer one or the other, right or wrong, the mind cease to exist. When the mind ceases to exist, things cease to exist.

The subject gives rise to the object. When the object ceases, the subject follows. The object cannot exist without the subject. The subject cannot exist without the object.

In the emptiness the two are one and the same. Their origin is the emptiness. Within the emptiness, all is equal with no distinctions.

The Great Way is all encompassing, neither easy nor difficult. Those who live within dualism are wroth with fear and separation. In their haste to be first, they become last.

In seeking you will never attain it. The very act of seeking creates separation. As long as separation exists, attainment cannot be had. Cease to seek and separation vanishes. Let things be as they are and there is neither gain or lost.

When you are in harmony with the Great Way you are free from disturbances. Shackled by your thoughts, you lose the truth and become unbalanced and afflicted.

When you are afflicted your mind is troubled. So why cling to attachments and aversions? If you desire to stay in the Great Way, strive to be free of judgments and opinions.

To accept the world without judgment or opinion is to realize true enlightenment. The wise attach to no judgments or opinions. The foolish concerned themselves with the trivial.

There is only one Dharma for all Dharmas are born from the One. Separation comes from attachments of the ignorant. Using the mind to seek the mind is the greatest mistake.

Peace and trouble are born from thoughts. Enlightenment has no thoughts. All division, all dualities come from ignorant thinking and judgments.

Thoughts are like dreams or clouds in the sky. Only the foolish try to grasp them. Abandon all such thoughts of right or wrong; gain or lost.

If the eyes never sleep, dreams will cease. If the mind makes no distinctions, then things are as they are within the essence of the Oneness.

When the deep mystery of the essence of Oneness is understood, you are free of the entanglements of duality. When all things are seen as one, you return to your original nature and remain in harmony with the Great Way.

Contemplate the movement within the stillness and the stillness within the movement. Both movement and stillness disappear. When dualities disappear even Oneness disappears.

The absolute state doesn't adhere to rules or descriptions. The awaken mind at one with the Great Way ceases all doing.

Doubts and separation vanish. The truth is established within you. In an instance you are free from the bondage of duality. You are free from attachments. Attachments no longer cling to you.

All is emptiness; clear and self-illuminating. With no need to endeavor the mind; thinking, feeling, knowing and imagination are of no value.

In this world of non-duality, there is neither self nor other. To become complete is to become whole with the One.

There is no separation in non-duality nor is anything excluded. The enlightened of all ages have known this truth.

The truth is beyond any space or time, an eternity in an instance. Not here or there but everywhere, always within your sight.

Infinitely large or infinitely small, infinity is infinity. No distinctions, no differences, no definitions for infinity has no boundaries. So too is existence and non-existence.

Don't dwell in taking sides or in discussions. Reframe from contemplating grasping the ungraspable. One thing and all things move among themselves without need for attention or distinction.

To live within this truth, within this realization; is not to dwell on perfection or non-perfection. To trust the Way is to live without separation. Within this non-duality you are one with the Way.

The Great Way is beyond language, words cannot grasp the Great Way.

CHAPTER THREE- TAO TE CHING

A Translation by Dennis Waller

Verse 1

The Tao that can be spoken is not the true Tao.

The names that are given do not contain their true meaning

Within the nameless is the true meaning

What is named has a mother and she is the mother of ten thousand things

The un-seeable is always seeable within the internal to those who are not bound by desire

Those who live in a state of desire see only the external illusion of manifestation

These two opposites are born from the same source
The source contains its mystery in darkness

Within the darkness is the darkness that is the gateway to the mysteries

Verse 2

All that is on the Earth residing under the Heavens that is beautiful is only beautiful because of the ugliness that coexists with the beautiful

There can be only good if there is evil

Difficult is the opposite of easy therefore they complement each other

The long and the short are related

The high and the low are related

Song and words are related

The front and the back are related

This relationship is the balance of the world as they come and go

The Sage is able to do without doing, teach without speaking

The ten thousand things come and go without interruption

Life and death, creating without possessing, staying in balance with nature

Accomplishing without taking credit, moving forward forgotten.

Therefore lives forever

Verse 3

Desiring not to possess or accumulate which is only temporal

Desiring not to covet the treasures of the world

These actions prevents temptation- stealing, jealously, ambition and quarreling

These actions keep the heart and mind pure.

The Sage with a pure heart and mind is at one with the Tao

Therefore free from the trappings of the world he is able to show the way

By emptying their hearts of desire and keeping their bellies full.

The people are simple and free therefore the cunning and the clever cannot interfere

All may live in peace and balance where there is action without interference

Verse 4

The Tao is like a vase that is empty yet used

It is the emptiness that gives birth to the vase

This emptiness, deep and unfathomable, is the source of the ten thousand things

It dulls the sharp

Unties the knots

Softens the light

Subdues the chaos

While hidden always present

Not knowing the source or from where it came, it has always been here since before time, for it is timeless

Verse 5

Heaven and Earth act without intention or
benevolence and are not moved or swayed by
offerings of straw dogs

The Sage acts in accordance to the same laws of
nature and is not moved by offerings of straw dogs

For nature follows the Tao and so the Sage, all is
equal under the sun, all is treated without regard or
condition, offering his gifts to all

Heaven and Earth are like bellows, empty yet
inexhaustible

As the work of the bellows is increased, so is the
production increased

Through these actions the Sage remains tranquil and
centered, sitting quietly while seeing the truth within
So with you.

Stay centered with your thoughts

Verse 6

The valley spirit never dies

For she is the mystic divine mother containing the perfection of the universe.

In all the forms of the mystic divine mother, her essence is never changing

For she is the gateway to all creation from which Heaven and Earth were born, her power always remaining unbroken

In the silence you will hear her without fail

In the stillness she will reveal her mysteries

Draw upon her wisdom as drawing water from a well, gently as her well is everlasting

Verse 7

The Heaven is everlasting and the Earth last forever
Why is this so?

For the Heaven and Earth does not exist for its own
sake

This is their secret

Like the Heaven and Earth, the Sage too lives the
same, putting himself last

By doing so, the Sage becomes first, through being
unselfish and serving the needs of others

Fulfillment is assured

Verse 8

The highest good is like water

Water brings life to ten thousand things, bringing nourishment without striving.

It seeks out the lowest levels to settle, places that people avoid and despise

This is like the Tao; water is in accordance with nature

The Sage is like water, living his life in accordance with nature, going with the flow of life.

The Sage seeks humble refuge, in meditation staying true without desire.

He is thoughtful in his relations with his fellow man, keeping an open heart

The Sage is gentle in his nature, standing by his word and actions, sincerity and honestly precedes him in his travels and dealings.

Always governing with equality, being timely and competent in his endeavors

Staying in balance and harmony with nature, the

Sage lives the way of the Tao

Verse 9

Better to stop pouring before the brim of the cup, for it is easier to hold an unfilled cup than a cup that is overflowing

Sharpen a sword to its sharpest edge and the edge will soon grow dull

Fill your house with gold and jade and you'll find it hard to protect

To desire fame, wealth, and honor is to bring about a downfall of your own doing

When your work is done, then retire

The Sage seeks neither fame nor fortune

Withdrawing once the work is done in a natural manner

This is the way of the Tao

Verse 10

Embrace your body and soul as one

How can you avoid the separation?

Can you allow your nature to be like that of a new born baby and be in harmony?

Can you begin to see with clarity the mystic vision?

Can you love your fellow man without judgment?

Can you rule the land without need of fame?

Playing the feminine part, can you open and close the gates of Heaven?

Can you see all throughout the land and people without interfering?

Can you control your Ego and stay within your authentic self?

Give birth and nourish without attachment,

To have without the need to possess.

To create and give without need of the credit,

Leading without being dominating.

Leading by example rather than rule

This is the mystical way of the Tao

Verse 11

Thirty spokes connect at the center of the wheel at the hub

It is the center of emptiness of the hub that makes the wheel useful

When shaping clay, it is the emptiness that creates the vase

It is in the emptiness that makes it useful

Rooms are made to have doors and windows

The usefulness of the room depends on what is not there

Without a door, a room cannot be entered

Without a window, there is no light

The usefulness of what exist depends on what doesn't exist

Such is the essence of non-existence

Verse 12

The five colors blind the eyes

The five sounds deafen the ears

The five flavors deaden the taste

Excessive desires will madden the mind

Excessive possessions preoccupy the mind with fear

The more you desire, the more you'll be discontented from what you have.

The Sage fills his belly, not his eyes

The Sage satisfies his inner desires with what cannot be seen, not with the external temptations of the world

Verse 13

Meet failure or success with grace, honor and kindness

Accept misfortune or fortune with grace, honor and kindness.

Why?

Do not be concerned with either.

Accept all that comes your way.

Good and evil comes from having a body, which is the cost of being human.

Good or evil cannot affect the true essence of the soul
The soul of man is everlasting.

Surrender yourself and love all that comes your way.

See yourself in all that comes your way

See the divine perfection in the Mother of the universe.

Know that you are one with all

In doing so you will be trusted to care for all things

Verse 14

What cannot be seen is invisible

What cannot be heard is inaudible

That which cannot be held is intangible

These three are beyond definition. Therefore they are as one

With no form or sound, they cannot be described

As they are from the nothingness that is unseen, unheard and untouchable

There is no light at rising.

There is no darkness at setting

It continues in a place where there is no time or space

Embrace it and you'll find no beginning or end

You cannot know it but you can be part of it

Embrace the experience beyond words and feel the essence of the Tao

Verse 15

The ancient masters of the Tao were subtle and mysterious

Their knowledge and wisdom was beyond that of the common man

It is difficult to describe these men, only by their appearance

Watchful and aware with no fear

Acting as a guest upon the earth in their travels

They were unpretentious, dignified, sincere, courteous, yielding, receptive, and pure of heart

Clarity comes to muddy waters by being stilled

In being tranquil in the stillness brings about peace from the chaos

The Sage of the Tao doesn't seek fulfillment therefore he is not affected by desires

Verse 16

Empty yourself completely

Bring your mind to rest and your heart to peace

Allow the ten thousand things to come and go while just observing

See how one ending is just another beginning

See the serenity in the movement to and fro from the divine source

Come to know the eternal wisdom by returning to the divine source and realize your destiny

For this is the enlightenment of the Tao

Knowing that all is everlasting

Even after the death of the body, you will remain whole in the Tao

Verse 17

The existence of the most exalted and revered leaders are barely known among men

Next comes the leaders who are loved and praised

Next comes those leaders who are feared and despised

A leader is trusted as much as he trust his fellow man

The exalted speaks little or carelessly

The exalted are wise in their words and actions

The exalted know the value of seeing their task completed by making it appear to have happened in a natural way

So the people will proclaim that the events happened by their own accord

The exalted have no need for praise or credit, no need to possess

Verse 18

When the great way of the Tao is forgotten

Benevolence and Righteousness will become prevalent

Then wisdom and logic will be born

Bringing about great pretense and hypocrisy followed by disorder

When harmony and balance cease to exist and man has lost his way

The virtue of caring for one another and love will arise from the chaos

At these times loyal servants will appear

Verse 19

If we could renounce and do away with wisdom, knowledge, religion and cleverness then it would be a hundred times better for everyone

Do away with morals and justice and people will begin to do the right things.

Give up the desire for wealth and thieves and robbers will disappear

These three forms of governing are insufficient

More important is living in a simple manner within one's own nature and keeping the well-being of others at heart

Living an unpretentious life with compassion and keeping your desires tempered is to live in your own true nature

This is the way of the Tao

Verse 20

Abandon learning to put an end to your troubles.

What is the difference between yes and no? What is the difference between good and evil? Are the fears of man truly merited? Or is it all nonsense?

In the spring some go to the park and enjoy a feast,

While I wander about alone not knowing where I am,

Like a newborn child who has yet to smile their first smile

I am alone belonging nowhere, unattached and homeless.

Others have too much, more than they need, striving for fame and fortune,

While I have nothing, embracing the shadows and relishing the solitude

Others are full of intellect and knowing with their cleverness and cunning,

While I am dumb and dull and play the fool with no worries or concerns.

I drift about like a wave on the ocean or like a cloud in the sky while everyone is consumed with their daily life

But I am different For I am nourished by the great mother

Verse 21

The greatest virtue is to be one with the Tao

Not by doing but being, not by striving but by thriving
The Tao is ever elusive and obscure

While vague and elusive it is seeable in its actions

Even though it is dim like the twilight, the essence of
the Tao shines

This essence is omnipresent, ever knowing and
everlasting

From the beginning before the beginning until now
and forever

Creation never ceases, always unfolding, always
being

I know this certainty because the Tao is within me

Verse 22

Yield like water and overcome

Bend like a Palm tree to remain straight.

Be empty like a vase to be full.

Death brings rebirth

To have little leaves room for more.

Those who have too much are troubled.

The Sage embraces humility to serve as an example for his fellow man

The Sage is free from the desire of needing recognition.

Therefore his example shines brightly.

His distinction comes not by force or assertion

He is powerful not by ruling with a heavy hand.

He is chief in not having pride.

He doesn't compete therefore no one can compete with him.

The ancient Sages say "Yield to overcome"

Stay whole and all things will come to you

Verse 23

To speak little is natural

High winds do not last the morning.

Thunderstorms do not last all day

Why is this so?

It is the Heaven and Earth

If the Heavens above and the Earth below cannot make these things eternal

Then how can man?

The one that follows the Tao is always one with the Tao

The one that is virtuous knows virtue by experience.

Those who don't follow the way of the Tao are lost and feel abandoned

Those who follow the way of the Tao are embraced by the Tao.

Those who are at one with virtue will always have virtue with them.

Those who are lost are embraced by abandonment

Those who cannot trust themselves will not be trusted by others

Verse 24

If you stand on your toes, you cannot stand in a steady fashion

If you run at an unnatural speed, you will not be able keep up the pace

One who brags of being enlightened is not

One that is self-righteous is not respected by others

Striving to bring attention to oneself for the sake of gain doesn't last and he will fall in despair

To the followers of the Tao these traits of bragging, self-righteous, and striving are unnecessary and are considered excesses

Followers of the Tao have no need of these traits and will avoid them

Verse 25

There is something supreme and mysterious that has existed before the Heaven and Earth

In the silence and solitude ever unchanging and ever present.

Ever extending and ever reaching is the mother of ten thousand things

Her name I know not.

This is called the Tao.

For the Tao is great.

Being great it flows out far away, only to return again. For this is the life breath of all things

The Tao is great, the heaven is great, the earth is great, the people are great

Here lie the four great powers of the universe with man being one of the great things.

Man follows the earth, the earth follows heaven and heaven follows the Tao

And the Tao follows its own nature of being the Tao

Verse 26

Gravity is the foundation for light

Stillness is the master of movement

The Sage that travels the day does not lose sight of his belongings

Along the way there are beautiful things to see but the Sage remains detached and stays indifferent choosing to keep his inner peace

Why should a king of ten thousand chariots not take his acts seriously?

For not to take ones duty with sincerity is to lose one's foundation

Not to practice stillness is to lose one's control

Verse 27

A Sage is a skilled traveler leaving no trace of his tracks

A Sage is a skilled speaker leaving nothing to be corrected in his words.

A Sage is like a skilled accountant needing no audit.

A Sage is like a door made pure needing no lock for it cannot be opened.

For what a Sage can bind cannot be unbounded

Therefore the Sage is always skillful in helping his fellow man, abandoning no one.

He is the caretaker of all things, abandoning nothing

This is the way of the Tao.

A good man is a teacher to the bad man.

A bad man is a student for the good man

If there is no honor for the teacher or for the student then confusion will arise no matter how clever the confusion is disguised.

Therefore this is the essence of the mystery

Verse 28

Know the strength of a man while keeping the essence of a woman

Keep your mind like a stream and let virtue flow unimpeded.

Be like a child free from the illusions of the world

Know the white by knowing the black.

Be an example of virtue to the world.

Be an example to the world to see and follow

Staying true without wavering and stay ever unchanging.

Staying on the path returning to the infinite.

Practice honor but keep your humility, living in the Tao

Become the valley of the world where virtue flows, ever true and ever flowing returning to the simple way of nature like an uncarved block

When an uncarved block is carved, it becomes useful.

When the Sage uses it he becomes a ruler.

Therefore a great tailor cuts little

Verse 29

Those who try to take over the world and rule it in an unnatural way end in failure

The world is sacred and fragile following the way of nature

The way of nature is the way of the Tao.

Therefore you cannot improve upon nature

Those who try to change it in the end destroy it. Those who try to grasp it cannot hold it

The way of nature is such that things sometimes are in front and sometimes behind

Sometimes strong and sometimes weak, sometimes hot and sometimes cold

Therefore the Sage avoids the extremes and does away with extravagance and indulgence

Verse 30

Those who instruct rulers of the world in the way of the Tao does so by being opposed to conquest by battle or arms

For battle begets battle, force begets force.

Thorns and briars follow in the footsteps of marching armies

Violence brings only more violence.

Battle, conquest, and force is not the way of nature

The Wise field commander who achieves his adjective does not continue.

He only strikes as a necessity, not for the glory or to boast.

He strikes only as a last resort, not for pride

Always guarding himself against being arrogant or displaying vanity.

For he knows these things are not the ways of nature.

Those who go against the way of nature will perish
The way of nature is the way of the Tao.

For what goes against the Tao is assured an early death

Verse 31

Weapons of war represent fear among men and are hated by all creatures

Followers of the Tao detest the use of them.

The wise leader considers the left to be honorable

While mongers of war prefer the right. Weapons of war are not for the wise

The wise only uses these weapons when it cannot be avoided.

The wise practice restraint and caution in the use of them.
Never does the wise see glory in their use

Those who relish and celebrate in the killing have lost their way of the Tao.

The act of war is like a funeral and should be mourned as such with sorrow and grief

Even for the victorious there should never be rejoicing for there is no good in this type of death

Verse 32

The ever unchanging Tao has no name.

Though it is small, simple, and subtle it cannot be grasped

If the kings and leaders could grasp the meaning of the Tao then the ten thousand things would obey their commands,

Heaven and Earth would become united and a gentle rain would fall without judgment towards anyone

Man would become free from the need of laws as all men would live in harmony with nature

Once the one becomes divided there is a need for naming all the parts.
There are already too many names

Knowing when to stop frees one from failure and trouble.

The Tao of the world is like a river flowing back to the great sea of divine source

Verse 33

Wisdom is in knowing others

Enlightenment is in knowing yourself

Force is required to overcome others

Strength is required to overcome yourself

Those who are content with their wealth are rich in the knowing of the Tao

Those who live their purpose live long

Those who live in the Tao live forever

Verse 34

The great Tao is everywhere, both to the left and to the right

The Tao gives all to the ten thousand things denying none

In fulfilling its purpose the Tao makes no claim or makes any assumption of being the lord of the ten thousand things,

Instead the Tao remains silent in its works

The ten thousand things always return to the Tao knowing that the Tao isn't their lord

By not showing greatness is truly great

The Sage is like the Tao, by not making himself great his greatness is attained

Verse 35

The Sage that is one with the Tao is at peace and will have the world come to him

Those who are in the presence of the Sage will experience the peace, calmness and happiness of the Tao

Music and merriment are only passing pleasures yet people partake of such festive activities but how empty and hollowed compared to the Tao

When you look for it, you cannot see it, when you try to hear it, it cannot be heard but when you use it, it is beyond being exhausted

Verse 36

That which is to be contracted first must be expanded

That which would be weakened must first be strong

That which would fall down must first be raised above

That which would be taken must first be given

This is the nature of things

The weak overtakes the strong, the soft overcomes the strong

Like fish that should not leave the water

Neither should the weapons of a country be displayed

Verse 37

The way of the Tao is non-action, always centered in stillness

Yet nothing is left undone

If the rulers of the world knew the way then the ten thousand things would follow their path according to the way of nature

For when things are simple, they return to the simplicity of formless nature

Without form there is no desire

Without desire there is peace in the stillness

Within this stillness is the natural way of the world

Verse 38

A man of virtue who is not aware of his virtue is truly a man of virtue.

A foolish man who tries to be of virtue is not a man of virtue

A man who is truly wise and of virtue seems to do nothing but leaves nothing undone.

The foolish man who is always trying to do, leaves much undone.

The man of virtue acts without regard to himself or with condition

The highest form of kindness is that which is given without regard to himself or without condition.

The highest form of morality is that which has no judgment or motive

When the Tao is lost then there is virtue.

When Virtue is lost then there is morality.

When Morality is lost then there is ritual

Ritual is only an empty shell of humanity like a flower and not the fruit; this is the beginning of the downfall of man

The great Sage follows his own nature and not that of society, following the fruit not the flower, he stays with the truth while rejecting the false

Verse 39

These things from the ancient times come from the one. The sky is whole and clear because of being of the one. The earth is whole and firm because of being of the one. The spirit is whole and complete because of being of the one

The ten thousand things are whole because of the one.

Kings and rulers are whole and the land is kept whole.

All these things are virtuous from being in the one.

The one being the Tao

If the sky wasn't so it would fall. If the earth wasn't so it would cave in. If the spirit wasn't so it would falter.

The rebirth of the ten thousand things prevent their death, Kings and rulers keep the virtue of the lands by it. Therefore being humble is the foundation of greatness.

The low is the foundation of the high. Kings and rulers call themselves "orphaned," "worthless," and "alone"

Is this an admission on their part of being humble? The individual parts of a carriage does not define a carriage for a carriage is more than the total of its parts.

The Sage does not wish to be seen as jade rather to be seen as common stone

Verse 40

Returning is the way of the Tao

Yielding is the way of the Tao

The ten thousand things are born of being

Being is born of non-being

Verse 41

When the wise student hears of the Tao, he practices it with sincere earnest.

When the student in the middle hears of the Tao, he may or may not follow the teaching

When a foolish student hears of the Tao, he mocks it, making fun of it with ridicule.

If the fool doesn't mock and ridicule it then it would not be the Tao

The path of enlightenment seems dark.

Going forward appears to be moving backwards

The easy way seems to be hard.

Virtue appears to be hollow.

Strength seems weak.

The great square has lost its corners

Great powers often come late.

Great music is hard to hear.

The greatest of all has no form.

The Tao is obscure and is without name.

The Tao is the nourishment that fulfills everything

Verse 42

The Tao produce the one

The one brought two and the two brought three.

It is the three that brought the ten thousand things

The ten thousand things are in the shadow and in the light

By the breath of these two harmony is brought into being

Man doesn't like to be "orphaned," "worthless," and "alone"

Yet this is how kings and rulers describe themselves

For in gaining, one loses.

For in losing, one gains

What others teach, I also teach,

A violent man will die a violent death.

This is the essence of my teachings

Verse 43

The weakest of things in the universe can overcome the strongest of things in the universe

That which has no substance can enter where there is no room

I know this is the value of non-action

Few are those who understand teaching without words or work without doing

Verse 44

What is most important?

Is it fame or life?

What is more treasured?

Is it wealth or life?

What is more painful?

Is it gaining or losing?

The man attached to fame and wealth will suffer

By gaining the man will still lose

The man contented is free from shame and danger and never disappointed

A contented man who practices restraint will be safe in all of his years

Verse 45

The greatest perfection seems imperfect yet its purpose cannot be exhausted

The greatest fullness seems empty yet it is ever endless

The greatest straightness seems crooked

The greatest intelligence seem stupid

The greatest eloquence seems awkward

Action overcomes the cold

Stillness overcomes the heat

Stillness, purity, and humility makes everything right in the order of the universe

Verse 46

When the Tao is practiced in the world, horses haul manure

When the Tao is discarded from the world, horses are used in war

The greatest sin for man is desire

The greatest misfortune for man is discontentment

The greatest violation for man is coveting that of others

Therefore the man being in a state of contentment is always contented

Verse 47

Without going outside the Sage knows everything that is outside

Without looking out the window he knows the Tao under the heavens

The farther one goes from himself the less he knows

Therefore the Sage has his knowledge without the need of traveling

Giving the right names to those things he doesn't see

He accomplishes his purpose without doing

Verse 48

He who is devoted to learning strives to increase his knowledge everyday

He who is devoted to the Tao seeks to decrease his doing everyday

He does less and less until there is nothing left to do

Once he has achieved non-action, there is nothing which he does not do

All things on earth are ruled by letting them follow their own nature

Things cannot be ruled, nothing can be gained by interfering

Verse 49

The Sage is not mindful of himself.

Rather he is mindful of the needs of others

To those who show goodness to me, I reply with goodness

To those who show evilness to me, I reply with goodness

For virtue is goodness.

Those who are faithful, I have faith in them

Those who are not faithful, I have faith in them
For virtue is faithfulness.

The Sage is humble and appears indifferent and impartial

People everywhere look upon and listen to the Sage

For the Sage hears and sees like a little child

Verse 50

Men come upon the earth to live and die

Three in ten will follow life.

Three in ten will follow death.

Three in ten will just pass through from birth to death, some barely here and others are born to disappear

What is the reason for this?

Because they live in their ego, not knowing their authentic self

The man who is aware of the Tao and walks in the Tao knows his authentic self and lives life with the laws of nature without fear or concern

In battle, he cannot be brought down by weapons.

In conflict, he cannot be harmed by adverse actions.

Not by a tiger or a rhinoceros can harm come to him How is this possible?

For death cannot enter him as he is above and beyond death.

His life is eternal for he lives in the Tao

Verse 51

All things are created by the Tao and are nourished by virtue

Things take their shape according to their nature

The ten thousand things honor the Tao and are grateful for virtue

Not because it is required by the Tao but freely given because this is the nature of things

Therefore it is the Tao that creation comes from.

By virtue all things are nourished and cared for

They are sheltered and protected from harm's way, allowing things to grow to completion

While the Tao creates, it doesn't claim to possess, without taking any credit

Leading by not interfering.

This is the way of the Tao

Verse 52

The Tao which was here before the beginning is considered the mother of all things

Knowing the mother you will know her children.

Knowing the children is to embrace the mother.

Embracing the mother brings freedom from the fear of death

Go within and guard your outer senses and have everlasting life in peace.

Lose your inner self and you'll lose control of your life The secret of clarity is having the perception of the small.

The secret of strength is having the perception of what is soft and tender

He who uses his wisdom of these laws learns to go within himself.

Within himself he is safe from harm for he is living in the eternal

For the bright light of the eternal is ever unchanging and free from evil.

Learning this principle is to live the Tao

Verse 53

If I have only the smallest amount of knowledge of the Tao.

I will walk the path of the Tao with my only fear being that of straying away

Keeping to the path is easy but people are distracted by the glamour on the side of the path

The royal court is draped in splendor and elegance but the fields lay bare with weeds and the stores are empty, void of provisions for the masses

The court wears elegant clothing carrying sharp swords indulging themselves in food and drink while the poor go unclothed and unfed

They have more possessions than they can use depriving those less fortunate.

The ones who boast of this wealth are the thieves and robbers

This is not the way of the Tao

Verse 54

The Tao is like a tree with deep roots, it is hard to pull up and bring down

The Tao is like what is firmly held in your grasp, it cannot slip away easily.

The Tao that is held and practiced will be honored from generation to generation

Learn to cultivate virtue in yourself and virtue will become you.

Learn to cultivate virtue in your family and it will grow.

Learn to cultivate virtue in the nation and virtue will become abundant.

Learn to cultivate virtue in the universe and virtue will be omnipresent

This is the effect of the Tao, from the greatest to the smallest, the Tao is there.

As above so below, change the outer by changing the inner, this is the Tao

How do I know the universe behaves this way?

By simply looking

Verse 55

He who is abundantly consumed with virtue is like a newborn child free from the sting of an insect

Or the fear of an attack from a beast or worried about the claws of birds of prey

Like a newborn child, his bones are soft and his muscles weak but his grasp is strong.

The union of man and woman is unknown to him but yet he is complete because he is at his height of vital force

He can cry all day without becoming hoarse as he is in harmony with himself.

Experiencing harmony is constancy. Experiencing constancy is enlightenment

It is not wise to rush about from here to there or trying to control the breath as it only causes unnecessary strain.

Exhaustion is caused by doing too much

Whoever behaves in this manner will have their years reduced for it is not natural

This is not the way of the Tao

Verse 56

Those who know do not speak. Those who do speak do not know

He that knows will keep his mouth closed and will keep guard of his senses

Blunt your sharpness, temper your emotions, smooth your rough edges, damper your brightness

Entertain stillness until you become one with the dust of the earth.

This is primal union, the mysterious unity

The Sage that has achieved this state of union is not bothered by profit or lost, kindness or meanness, honor or disgrace,

Nor does he knows the difference between friend or foe

This form of detachment is the highest form for man for he is the noblest one under heaven

Verse 57

To be a great leader you must follow the Tao.

Wage war only if there are no other options.

The world is ruled by non-interference. How do I know this?

By this-

With more laws and regulations the people become poorer.

The more weapons a kingdom possesses, the greater the level of strife among the people

With disorder the more disingenuous and corrupt men become,

The more strange things take place requiring more laws and regulations hence more thieves and robbers

Therefore the Sage teaches.

By practicing non-action the people are reformed.

Out of the stillness of peace comes honesty.

In doing nothing the people will prosper on their own accord

By having no desires the people will return to living a natural life, a life that is simple and good

Verse 58

When a country is ruled justly with a light hand the people are simple and good

When a country is ruled with force and a heavy hand, the people become cunning and discontented

Misery is hidden within happiness

Happiness is hidden within misery.

Who knows when and how this will end?

When the honest people become dishonest then evil grows for the people are mislead

Therefore the Sage is sharp without cutting in his teachings

Pointed without piercing people.

He is straightforward with being disrupting.

And is not blinding with his brilliance

Verse 59

It is best to practice moderation and restraint in the governing of people and in the care of nature

Restraint begins with being unselfish and not putting yourself first

Your ability to succeed is based on the virtue that you have stored

If you have accumulated a good store of virtue then nothing is impossible

When nothing is impossible then there are no limits

When a man has no limits, then he is poised to be a great leader

This is from having deep roots and a firm foundation in the way of the Tao

The Tao offers a long fruitful life with inner vision to the eternal

Verse 60

Governing a country is like cooking a small fish

Let the country be ruled by the way of the Tao and evil will have no power over the land

It isn't that evil doesn't have power; it is because the way of the Tao protects those who follow it against the way of evil

Like the Sage who harms no one, virtue is allowed to prosper for all the people

Verse 61

A great country is like a stream in the low lands, allowing all to flow to the stream for this becomes the center from which all things in the universe can be ruled, this is the mother of all things

It is in the stillness and quietness that the mother is able to overcome the male

Through this stillness and quietness a great country can overcome a small country

By this principle a small country can overcome a great country

The great succeed by yielding, the small by remaining humble

Verse 62

The source of the ten thousand things is the Tao.

The Tao serves as a treasure for man and as a safe haven for the lost

If someone is lost, offer fine words to awaken him, offer good deeds to him, repay his unkindness with kindness.

Do not discard the man but do discard his evil wayward ways

Let your gift to him be living in the way of the Tao

Therefore on the day a leader is elected, do not offer your expertise or wealth to him.

Rather help him by staying in the way of the Tao and teach him the way of the Tao.

Let your way serve as an example for him to follow
The ancients prized this way in the days of old.

It wasn't because the Tao is the source of all good or the cure for evil.

But because it is the most noble thing to do thus making it the greatest treasure in the universe

Verse 63

Practice non-action, work without doing and taste the tasteless.

Treat the insignificant with significance; embrace the kind and unkind alike, treating both with the same kindness

See the simplicity in the complicated, see the greatness in the small things and act accordingly

In nature the difficult things are done in an easy manner, great things are made up by the acts of small things; this is the nature of nature, achieving greatness with no effort.

This is the law of natural progression

The Sage is like nature in achieving greatness by practicing the law of natural progression in doing small acts to obtain greatness.

Promises made without regard to sincerity are often unfulfilled

Treating easy things in life without sincerity often turn them into difficult things.

Because the Sage stays on the path of the Tao and practices the laws of nature by approaching all things with sincerity, he never experiences these problems of life

Verse 64

What resides in stillness is easily managed.
Evil can be eliminated before it has formed.
The fragile is easily broken. The insignificant can
become lost.

Confront issues before they become issues. Put
things in order before there is disorder.

The largest of trees started life as a sapling. A nine
story building began with a single brick. A journey of
ten thousand miles begins with a single step.

By acting it is destroyed, by grasping, it is lost
The Sage doesn't act therefore is not defeated, by not
grasping, he doesn't lose

People fail often nearing the end; as much care is
needed at the end as it is in the beginning.

By giving careful thought from beginning to end,
failure is prevented

The Sage has no desires or ambitions for those things
difficult, he is detached from precious things and
holds on to no ideas

He brings men who are lost back to the way of the
Tao,

He assists the ten thousand things in their natural
progression and he does this by non-interference

Verse 65

In the days of old, the ancients that followed the Tao did not try to enlighten the masses

But kept them in ignorance for it was easier to rule with the people who were simple

The more the people know the harder it is to govern them because of their cleverness.

Hence when the king tries to rule with cleverness the country is brought into misfortune

A country that is not ruled by cleverness is brought into good fortune and the land is blessed for the people are simple

The ability to know these two ways of governing and choosing to rule without cleverness is to know the mystic virtue

The mystic virtue is deep rooted and far reaching.

It brings all things back into harmony leading them to unity and to the great oneness of the universe

Verse 66

The great sea is the King to all the streams and rivers of the world.

All streams and rivers flow into the great sea
.

His kingdom is given its power by being below them all

So is the way of the Sage, leading by being behind, by serving in a humble manner

In this approach the people are not threatened or feel oppressed by him.

By ruling as a servant the people choose to have him as their king.

By this way the people never grow tired of the Sage knowing that no harm can come to them

Because he doesn't compete, there is no competition to meet

Verse 67

Everyone in the world talks about my Tao with such familiarity as to its greatness.

Because of its greatness it is different from all other teachings thus making it look like a folly

The Tao is not something to be bought or sold at the marketplace, or something that can be put into a box and given away.

If this was so then the Tao would have been lost and forgotten years ago.

There are three treasures that I hold and keep

The first is unconditional love, the second is frugality; the third is one not putting oneself ahead of others

From unconditional love comes courage.

From frugality comes generosity.

From not putting oneself ahead of others come leadership

Courage without unconditional love, generosity without frugality, forcing oneself upon people will end in failure

In battle unconditional love will be victorious and will firmly hold its ground.

By this very act of unconditional love the heavens will guard those and grant protection to them

Verse 68

A good soldier is not prone to violence

A good fighter is not prone to rage

A good winner is not boastful of his victory

A good employer is humble in serving his employees
This is the embodiment of virtue

It is the way of non-striving, non-competing, and being humble.

Being a master of these traits is to know how to use your fellow man to the best of his abilities, allowing him to shine brightly

This has been known since the days of old as a unity of heaven and earth

Verse 69

The masters of war have a saying

"I do not dare to be the host; rather I wish to be the guest,

I do not dare advance an inch, rather I wish to retreat a foot"

This is called marching with the appearance of not moving, rolling up a sleeve without showing an arm, conquering the enemy without attacking.

Being armed without weapons

The greatest disaster in war is underestimating the enemy

Underestimating the enemy can cost you your treasures

And cost you those things that are dearest to you

In battle the victory will go to the one who is the most compassionate

Verse 70

My words are easy to know and easy to practice yet few men on earth know of these words and even less are practicing these words

My words are from the times of the ancients, my deeds have a Prince.

Since no one knows this, I am to remain unknown.

Those who do know me are few and far in between
And those who do know me should be respected.

Knowing me is like having the treasure of jade

Therefore the Sage walks among men with the treasure of jade kept hidden within himself

He covers his body with the rags of a beggar in order to hide the treasure.

This the way of the Sage

Verse 71

Having an awareness of ignorance is to know strength

Casting aside ignorance is a disease

Only when we realize that we are riddled with disease do we know that we are sick

Once we become sick of being sick will we be able to move towards health

The Sage is always in a state of health.

His secret is that he chooses health not disease or sickness

Verse 72

When men no longer have a sense of awe, disaster will follow

Men will begin to look outward from themselves for guidance

For they will no longer trust themselves

In this guidance they will be led astray by a clever ruler

Therefore the Sage doesn't enter their homes and he doesn't interfere with their work

The Sage chooses non-interference so the people will not be confused.

He doesn't bring attention to himself rather keeping his self-respect without showing arrogance.

In not exalting himself the Sage chooses to let go of that which he has no need of

Verse 73

A man of bravery and passion acting without the Tao
will be killed or will kill

A man of bravery and calmness acting with the Tao
will always preserve life.

Of which of these two men is in grace and which is
lost?
Not all things on earth are favored by heaven.

Why is this so?

Even the Sage doesn't know all the answers under
heaven

Heaven is always at ease, succeeding by not striving.
By not striving it overcomes

It doesn't speak yet it is answered.

It comes without being called.

It achieves its goals without effort.

It doesn't ask yet all is provided.

Seemly still it moves with ease.

Heavens net covers the universe, while the net is
coarse and wide, nothing slips through

Verse 74

When you realize that all things are constantly changing then you surrender to trying to hold on to anything

When you realize that death is nothing more than an illusion then your fear of death disappears

Men who live in fear of death are afraid of breaking the laws that result in death.

Who would dare break such a law that results in death?

There is an official executioner that is responsible for death.

Choosing to take his position is like a novice of carpentry trying to work wood like the master carpenter,

Harm will come to your hand by not knowing the use of the tools.

Verse 75

When the government taxes are too high, people will go hungry

When the government invades the lives of the people, the people will lose their spirit

Therefore act in the best interest of the people

Trust them and leave them alone

Verse 76

When a man is born he is soft, gentle and weak.

Upon his death he has become hard and stiff

Green plants are the same as man, when young they are supple and tender.

At their death they are dry and withered.

Therefore the path of death is unyielding, hard, and stiff whereas the path of life is flexible, soft and supple.

An army that is unyielding and unable to be flexible is assured to be defeated

The hard and unyielding will be defeated

The soft and flexible will succeed

Verse 77

The way of the Tao of heaven is like drawing back a bow. The top is brought down while the bottom is brought up. Like the Tao, the bow takes what is abundant and gives to where there is a need. This way the bow maintains balance and harmony.

This is the way the Tao behaves throughout the universe. Keeping balance and harmony by taking from an overabundance and giving to where there is a deficiency.

Only the Sage acts in accordance with this law for the ways of man are different.

The way of man is to take from those who don't have enough to give without having regard to their well-being. He uses force to control his fellow man.

Desires keep men discontented and in want of more. Rampant ambitions rule their decisions in order to feed their greed.

Who can go against this way and instead share his abundance with the world? Only a man that follows the way of the Tao can perform these feats.

Therefore the Sage gives without needing recognition, serves without bringing attention to his actions, he achieves without the need of reward.

Once his work is accomplished he moves on. He shows no desire except to help others for this is his wisdom.

Verse 78

There is nothing in the world that is weaker or softer than water and yet when it attacks things that are strong and hard,

There isn't anything better or more effective than water to create change.

It is the weakness that gives water its strength.

The soft can overcome the hard; the gentle can overcome the harsh. While men know this law, very few practice it.

Therefore the Sage says:

Only the one that can carry the burden of men, to take their shame upon himself is worthy to lead his fellow countrymen.

Living in serenity amongst the sorrow, free from the evil that abounds, only he can lead the people in a just manner.

The truth often seems paradoxical.

Verse 79

When a settlement is reached between two parties where there is great animosity there is bound to be a bitter grudge held by the party that felt he was wronged.

How can these thoughts be of benefit to the other?

Therefore the Sage knowing of the bitter grudge will keep the left hand side of the agreement, making no claim on anyone, and will not request a fast settlement from the other party.

He will repay unkindness with kindness for this is the way to end the hostility.

For the Sage is with virtue.

A man of virtue gives while a man absent of virtue takes.

Verse 80

When a country is governed with the Tao the citizens are contented

They enjoy the fruit of their labor without the need of machines to save time.

Their love for their home is so deep that they do not desire to travel.

While there are carts and boats, they go nowhere.

They may have weapons stored but there is no use for them.

They are a happy and simple group that enjoys their food and families ensuring that the needs of the neighborhood are cared for.

Their clothing and homes are simple and they live in peace.

Even though they are so close to their neighboring country that the barking of dogs and the crowing of the cocks can be heard,

They still have no desire to go, rather staying content to die in their homes of old age having lived a life in peace, love and happiness.

Verse 81

Truthful words are not always beautiful

Beautiful words are not always true

The wise do not argue to prove a point.

The men that argue their point are not wise

The Sage doesn't seek to acquire for himself, rather he desires to give to others

The more he gives, the more he has.

With this he continues to give more only to receive more.

The way of the Tao is to be giving and not harm

The Sage gives without striving; working without effort, thinking only of others

This is the way of the Tao.

CHAPTER FOUR- NAGARJUNA'S TREE OF WISDOM

A Translation by Dennis Waller

verse 1-

Evil people should be dealt with and placed under control. The wise should be held in reverence. Quest to fill your soul with honest deeds, And have compassion for your own countrymen

verse 2-

With regards to your own secrets and those of others, Guard these as your own dear child. For those for whom all earthly things are equal, Will have love in their heart for all men.

verse 3-

If your wife is evil and your friend evil, If the King is evil and your relatives evil, If your neighbor is evil and the country evil, Then abandon them and make haste for a distant land.

verse 4-

Avoid those who are greedy for wealth. Avoid a wife who is fond of fornication. Abandon these people and seek those of good morals. Be with those who are strong and virtuous.

verse 5-

Although you know the difference between good and bad deeds, You should carry out your actions after careful consideration. Although you may only partially succeed, You are to be admired for your purity of heart and mind.

verse 6-

The steadfast who speak with few words and politely, Are very much respected and admired by their peers. As the sun rises from the night and by his rays creates great heat, You too should let your actions speak highly of you

verse 7-

Though you may suffer for your convictions in the face of adversity, Be not anxious but steadfast in your heart and mind. As surely as the sun has set for the night, Will it not shine again in the morning?

verse 8-

As the gardener knows that it is mother earth that produces the flowers. While flowers are admired and loved, they are fleeting. Be not forgetful of the source of this beauty. In the same way, you should be like the root firmly planted.

verse 9-

Not ever compromise your morals and values for material gain, Whether it is for royal favor or rewards. For these are transitory and will vanish in time, But a good heart that is pure will last indefinitely.

verse 10-

Things not understood are to be avoided till they are clear. Be not indifferent to the concerns of health, liberty, or life. Be not indifferent to your obligations. Honor your obligations with due diligence.

verse 11-

Worthy men do not make many promises. But when a promise is made, It is made as if carved in stone, And to be honored even at the cost of death.

verse 12-

On occasion you will agree with your foes for the time is right. On occasion you'll disagree with your friends, and that time will be right. Learn to distinguish when you should and should not agree. The clever man will always seize opportunities when presented to him.

verse 13-

Be mindful of the words you speak. For words spoken cannot be retracted. Learn to accomplish through actions rather than speech. Conquer through silence rather than through senseless noise.

verse 14-

Preparedness is necessary in order to keep adversaries at bay. By being persistent at being prepared is to overcome. Ignorance is to assume that all will be well. This course of thought will result in being defeated.

verse 15-

Keep your thoughts to yourself as you would a secret, Thoughts made public are prone to be defended. Be strong and silent like the root. For it is the flower that gets cut.

verse 16-

Although you may witness beyond the veil in this world. Others cannot perceive pass the veil. Make no mention of this. Rather you would welcome to be ridiculed.

verse 17-

Be wary of any wolf wrapped in sheep's clothing. Know this disguise of evil well. For this evil is presented within niceties. Don't be brought to slaughter by a sweet song.

verse 18-

Impress upon others the thoughts you choose for them. Have them contemplate your thoughts. While believing that these thoughts are their own. This is the key to controlling men.

verse 19-

Be humble in your ways. Desire not the trappings of success. For earthy wealth brings misery and quarrelling. Life is easier being contented with little.

verse 20-

It is mankind's nature not to quarrel or war. Wealth obtained by quarrelling will soon be fleeting. Why would you choose to lose your soul for earthy wealth? Earthy wealth is nothing more than an illusion.

verse 21-

The foolish are those who fill their plate with more than they can eat, Those who continue to pour tea into their cup after it is filled, Whose eyes are larger than their mind and make their thoughts public. For these four traits are a living death.

verse 22-

Give no respect or thought to those who are evil minded, Not for a prince, not for deceitful family, Not for an unfaithful woman, For these are sinners who have cast their fate.

verse 23-

Hold no earthy attachments to your possessions. For the man consumed with possessiveness will suffer. Possessiveness and attachment bring with it greed. These's are traits of evil.

verse 24-

A man of much worldly knowledge has two forms of happiness. Either he will renounce attachment to worldly possessions, Or abandon with all earthly interest. Either way, he will experience true freedom.

verse 25-

When your glory has abandoned you, And your efforts have become meaningless. There is only one happiness for you. By returning and becoming one with nature.

verse 26-

The life of a wise and holy man is like that of a flower. Either to be admired by the masses. Or to be lost to the world. Like the flower on the forest floor.

verse 27-

Life that perishes naturally is a life that ends modestly. As so you should live, with a sense of moderation. For living with moderation has its essence. Especially if your intellect is not developed.

verse 28-

This is the thing to understand. The Law of Familiarity. Don't be too vocal or visual for this diminishes fear. The master knows the importance of balance of caring and not.

verse 29-

Like the moon from waxing to fullness, Like the bees making honey, Like the possessions of the wealthy Abundance comes from gradual accumulation.

verse 30-

Do not be excessively covetous or envious. When consumed with these desires, Pain and sorrow will surely follow. For this is the punishment of such actions.

verse 31-

Ensure you can protect the wealth you have conquered, Before going forward in acquiring more acquisitions. Don't be overcome by greed or lust for more. This action will result in the theft of your possessions by your neighbor.

verse 32-

Do not covet fame for it is hollow in its wisdom and knowledge. Be honest in judging yourself. Desires for such fame will take you off the path. Such fame will take you from your purpose.

verse 33-

Do not say things which will bring pain to others. Know that words are like swords that cut deeply. The word and sword are known as equals throughout the lands, And can equally kill in one stroke.

verse 34-

Be wary of sweet gifts of your enemy. Don't be overcome by outward beauty. The wise look at the essence of the gift before accepting. Adhering to this principle will avoid injury.

verse 35-

To the benefit of your enemy, be just in your intentions. Be guided by reason and truth in a compassionate manner. Then you'll see your enemies come before you with their hands folded. And bow to you in devotion.

verse 36-

Injure your enemy by kindness rather than conflict. Praise his good qualities and strengths. Know that whatever harm you hold within, Will injure you and not your enemy.

verse 37-

Be steadfast in dealing with those who don't conform. Use harsh measures if necessary. Be like a father to his own children. Does not the father threaten punishment against infractions?

verse 38-

As long as you stay on the path of the Way, As long as your steps are steady with commitment, As long as your wisdom is unimpaired, Your rewards will be beyond measure.

verse 39-

Be free from what is expected of you by the masses. To do this is to be free from them. Don't try to please everyone as this is impossible. Choose to honor yourself to have peace.

verse 40-

For the fool seeks what he doesn't know, Desires what he has no knowledge of, Bursting with pride while having no substance, For these traits make a fool.

verse 41-

Be careful who you befriend. Like the wind was befriended by the fire, It was the wind that brought death to the fire. Likewise weak men create their demise by the friends they choose.

verse 42-

Choose to do no harm to others, Choose not to let low people rule you. Choose to stay on the path of virtue. Choose not to abandon this principle.

verse 43-

Living a day in the Divine Love of the Way, Is greater than living a hundred years in worldly ways. Live not the ways of the world, Strive to live in the way of the Way.

verse 44-

When the weak minded come into wealth, They become consumed with greed and pride. When the virtuous attain wealth, They remain humble as the poor.

verse 45-

Worldly people are like lowly forms of life. Quarreling rules their days, Their greed blinds their sight, Peace is ever eluding.

verse 46-

When worldly people possess wealth, They become boastful and proud. The wise on the other hand stay steadfast, Even with wealth, they remain humble.

verse 47-

The virtuous doesn't engage in quarreling, nor being prideful. The virtuous doesn't use foul language, nor covet the flesh, Nor do they work without profit These are the not traits of the virtuous.

verse 48-

Those consumed by pride would rather suffer,
Than to admit being in need of assistance. In order to
maintain outwardly appearances, Suffering is
preferred rather than to succumb to asking for help.

verse 49-

There is a bird which lives off the morning dew. For
it fears the imprisonment of obligation. To have no
obligation to anyone, Is to have your freedom.

verse 50-

The enlightened have no need for a teacher. As the
cured have no need for a doctor. Once the water is
crossed, there is no need of the ferry. Once a task is
complete, there is no need to do it again.

verse 51-

Even an evil man, weak and in good nature, Can
be dealt with easily. And like calm waters, He
shouldn't be disturbed.

verse 52-

When people become unyielding in their beliefs,
And confrontations arise, There will be no ground for
compromise. How can this be of any benefit to
anyone?

verse 53-

When ego rules the conversation, Expect the discussion to be boisterous, By men filled with pride and arrogance. That gathering will bear no fruit.

verse 54-

Addictions rob the body, mind and soul of peace. Stay clear of such behavior. For it unsettles the mind And takes strength from the body.

verse 55-

The man filled with greed and selfishness, Is like a barking dog with no bite. He is of no benefit to anyone, Therefore, what is his purpose.

verse 56-

In times of misfortune, whether it is natural or by war, In times of distress, all are equal alike, A time of famine or danger from enemies, The king and the impoverished are affected the same.

verse 57-

People consumed with greed are never satisfied, They continue to strive for worldly possessions. This not natural for even a calf exhausting the milk, Will leave the mother cow and go to a distance.

verse 58-

To lose one's affection, the contempt of one's own people, To be much in debt, to be accused of wrongdoings, To be abandoned by friends who see your poverty, These five are not fire yet they burn the body the same.

verse 59-

Address problems as soon as they are born. Do not allow them to mature. As they are easy to defeat in infancy, They are hard to overcome at maturity.

verse 60-

He who has knowledge is firm and steadfast. The wise, even when destitute, keep to their virtues. Like the scorching heat of the sun's heat, The natural coldness of the snow remains.

verse 61-

Those who live in the Way live forever. Those who live in the flesh, die in the flesh. Those who are self-absorbed and live in conceit, Are already bound in damnation.

verse 62-

Those who live in the desire of sin are blind to the Way. As the blind cannot see the beauty of a sunset, Neither can the self-absorbed and greedy see the Way. Living in ego blinds one from seeing the real truth.

verse 63-

The subtle ways of water, the creeping vine, Turtles, and crafty women are the ways of, Small distinctions that bring success. For these subtle ways overcome adversity.

verse 64-

What goes around comes around, Like misery follows pleasure, And pleasure follows misery. This too will pass like the night into day.

verse 65-

Things come and go throughout life Make no attachments to any of them. With attachment comes pain and suffering Know that it is all an illusion.

verse 66-

As the sun rises and sits, So we will be born and die Have comfort in knowing this truth, That your essence is not affected by these actions.

verse 67-

The angry are defeated before the battle begins. Evil is brought upon evil by their actions. While the fool confronts evil with anger, The wise conquers by not being angry.

verse 68-

As a large stone can be rolled down the hill with little force, So can your ego be affected by the smallest distinction. Like that of the big oak tree, be firmly planted in the ground.

verse 69-

Leave be those things that are to be left alone. For engaging in these affairs will only bring grief. Like that of trying to grasp the clouds. Concern yourself with your own matters.

verse 70-

The man who meddles in the affairs of others, Will have despair as his guest in the evening. He that finds comfort in the misery of others, Will surely be brought down.

verse 71-

What does it benefit a man to know the affairs of his neighbors, While his own home is in disarray? Like the cat that is watched by the dog, The mouse is free to roam.

verse 72-

Thoughts become clear in a still mind Like the reflection of the moon on a calm pond. Clarity comes to the stillness. Practice stillness to know inner truth.

verse 73-

A mouse who undertakes any task, Whether it is large or small, With the intent of doing his best work, Will be met with the respect of the lion.

verse 74-

Many have met their death on assumption. At all times be certain of your actions. Rely not on others for your well being. Be vigil of your thoughts.

verse 75-

The man who acts out of love and compassion, Will be met with great success. One who lives in unconditional love, Will surely control his own fate.

verse 76-

By always uttering pleasant speeches, It is easy for a king to beguile his people. However meaningful words should have value like gold, Speak these words with the same rarity as gold.

verse 77-

Follow your own intuition. Even when it is not popular among others. Stay true to your truth. Even when confronted with those who appear more wise than you.

verse 78-

He that knows the power within his wealth and ability, Will prove to be a formidable foe, One to be avoided at all cost. His wrath is such that it has no equal.

verse 79-

If fire can burn in water, Then what can extinguish it? Fear born from within is like this fire. Protect yourself from fear and cast it out.

verse 80-

Even a drum when not properly tuned will produce ill sounds. Treat your world like a finely tuned drum to ensure sweet sounds. Be aware of this to preserve tranquility and peace. Not only for you but for those around you

verse 81-

Those who are self absorbed and greedy, Know not the distinction between causing pain and joy. All that matters are their own concerns, At the cost of others, is not their worry.

verse 82-

It is better to give freely what can be given, Rather risk lost of life and liberty. Like the sheep that have their fleece sheared, The essence of the sheep remain and the fleece will return.

verse 83-

When there is a snake at the root and an eagle above, Monkeys climbing in the branches and the flowers surrounded by bees, A resting place is provided for all of natures animals, Know that nature provides for all within its domain.

verse 84-

In battles of war, It is not the physical aspects that win, Rather it is the mental aspects that bring victory, Cunning and cleverness rule over brute strength.

verse 85-

Strength without cunning is worthless, Against an opponent that possesses cunning and cleverness. He who understands this is mighty. For even a lion can be brought down by a mouse.

verse 86-

Seek from those who possess the knowledge you desire. A journey started is better than one never attempted. Success is measured by the distance gained. Not in hope and wishes.

verse 87-

The actions of the virtuous speak louder than words. Words of worldly people bring no comfort. Follow the example of the master. This is the key for the student to learn.

verse 88-

Confront your fears head on with determination,
Rather than sulk in misery. Take the necessary
actions and control, Thus fears are conquered.

verse 89-

Live life free of the fear of the unknown, For there
is nothing to fear. Live life free of the fear of the
known, For you can conquer those fears.

verse 90-

Speak not of your cleverness to the deaf. Show not
your knowledge to the blind. Comfort not those who
do not seek comfort. Give not your food to those who
have no craving.

verse 91-

Resist the temptation to be proud, Not in your
youth, strength, or knowledge, Not in riches, wealth,
or health, Be humble in your thoughts and actions.

verse 92

Whatever harm you cause, you bring to yourself.
Whether man or beast, bring no harm onto either. To
practice this principle is to be one with the way.
Therefore like the sun, burning brightly for all to see.

verse 93-

Speaking in lies and falsehoods, Acting in an unbecoming manner, Not heeding your nature, These are the traits of a fool.

verse 94-

Seek to immerse yourself, In that which is wise and holy. By immersion you may become, Wise and holy.

verse 95-

Choose your moments to speak, For speaking at the right time ensures , That your words carry weight. By treating your words like gold, others will treasure them.

verse 96-

Patience and perseverance, Duty and honor, Wisdom and courage, Together bond a force that even the Gods fear.

verse 97-

Trust not your enemy, not even in defeat. More kings have been defeated by betrayal. Do not forget this principle, Or your fate will be that of the hare served for dinner.

verse 98-

Bodily functions and desires are the same for the ignorant and the wise. By the practice of the way, the ignorant can rise above. If the way is not understood, the ignorant will remain in darkness.

verse 99-

The ignorant that speak ill of the way, Are like day and night, They come and go. They may breathe but there is no life in them.

verse 100-

The ignorant that ignore the way, Are like those dying of thirst, While being next to a stream, They struggle to dig a well with no avail.

verse 101-

Although you may remain on vacation for a very long time, It is absolutely certain that you will have to return home. Whatever may be the circumstances. Returning home cannot be avoided.

verse 102-

Excessive pain is caused by attachment, When separation isn't accepted, But if it is voluntary by the act of letting go, Infinite peaceful happiness will be obtained.

verse 103-

One's desire is to be attractive and happy, And wealth is of course pleasant and natural. But yet this world of existence, Is but an illusion, temporary and fleeting.

verse 104-

Lust is the most detrimental of sins. Envy is the most harmful to others. Cunningness is a wolf in sheep's clothing. But Generosity has no equal in its purity.

verse 105-

There is no light like the light of wisdom. There is no darkness like that of spiritual darkness. The blindness to the way is the worse of blindness. Strive for the light of wisdom as wisdom has no equal.

verse 106-

As certain as the sun will rise tomorrow. So too will death come to you. With this knowing turn your mind from worldly thoughts, And rejoice while on the path of the Way.

verse 107-

Desire for earthly jewels has been the downfall of many. Temper your lust for these as their value is fleeting, Rather desire for the jewels of the divine. For these are the everlasting jewels of the Way.

verse 108-

The wise possess tranquility in abundance. For they know that the riches of the earth, Gold, cattle, grain, land, wealth, or health, None of these can sustain the soul forever.

verse 109-

Hoarding wealth brings great pain and suffering, In fears of it being stolen or lost. While entertaining at times, In the end it brings more misery than joy.

verse 110-

Nothing earthly is everlasting. Strive to acquire what is everlasting. Quest not to own earthly treasures, Rather seek those treasures of the divine.

verse 111-

A king is never satisfied with great wealth. A clever man is never fulfilled with hearing his words. Never is there enough beauty in the world for these men. These things are like the desires of a child, never satisfied.

verse 112-

Consume yourself with high morals and virtues. Composure, self-reliance, control over your thoughts. Whoever possesses these traits are contented, For what more do they need.

verse 113-

If you are fully contented with your life, You are far from the thoughts of evil. Desires of carnal pleasure bring with it troubles. This is the source of evil thoughts.

verse 114-

With all the faults of being human, There remains one great moral quality. And that is the power to choose, Choose wisely.

verse 115-

Strive to attain modesty and contentment, For these traits know not death. Like the elephant, powerful as it may be, Sustains on grass.

verse 116-

Is there really such a thing as personal property? Does not the light of the sun belong to everyone? Is not the air available for all to breathe? What use then is this personal property?

verse 117-

The surest possession is real contentment. It is not difficult to earn a living. Like nature, there is an abundance throughout. There is no place where it cannot be found.

verse 118-

Like nature where the tiger rules and the elephant is king. Make your place among the grass and trees. And eat the fruits of the trees. The ways of evil men and society are not a real life.

verse 119-

The man that accepts his fate, Whether good or bad, And keeps his heart and mind pure, Has no need of worldly wealth.

verse 120-

Your body is like a ship and your good actions, Are the winds that sail the ship, Over the ocean of human misery. So long as your ship is not wrecked.

verse 121-

As long as the moon shines and sun rises, And so long as death is on holiday, Keep chaste in your actions, And be pure of heart and mind.

verse 122-

Standing on the precipice of your death, On watching the sunset on your life as you leave, You'll make the journey alone as it should be. A wife or child will be of no assistance on this journey.

verse 123-

The man who can rejoice with contentment, Who can find happiness in simple things, And who lives in concert with nature, Upon discarding his body will have salvation.

verse 124

If your thoughts are motivated by wisdom, Then salvation is very near. For salvation comes from within, Not from wearing robes of ochre.

verse 125-

What does it avail a man to clothed his body? Feed his stomach and neglect his heart and soul? For the man that has the love of all living things, In his heart and soul has no need of robes of ochre.

verse 126-

He who is quiet in the prime of life, I know in order for this person to be quiet, If all the senses were completely exhausted by age, How could he possibly not be quiet?

verse 127-

As wood is transformed into smoke by the act of fire. So too is your soul when awakened to the Way. With this new change over you, strive to walk on the path, And practice acts of virtue along your way.

verse 128-

Wealth, acquired through theft, mischievous means, Or by acts not acceptable to the community, Or by betrayal of your neighbors, Such acquiring of wealth is not proper wealth.

verse 129-

Being concerned by what others think about you, Will only bring misery, for this is vanity. The man of virtue does not concern himself with such thoughts .By not discriminating one or the other, this man is happier.

verse 130-

He that has no sense of right or wrong, Or only concerns himself with himself, Who quest to fulfill only his own desires, What difference is there between this man and the beasts?

verse 131-

Knowledge is the great source of virtues. Both visible and invisible therefore should be desired. For to take hold of wisdom in its entirety, Requires that you accept both visible and invisible.

verse 132-

One out of a hundred is born a hero. One out of a thousand is born clever. One out of hundred thousand is born wise. But a wise hero may be born in one.

verse 133-

The wise never cease to quest to learn regardless of age, Even though there may be no benefits of it in this life. For this knowledge learned is not for naught, As it will be available to them in another life.

verse 134-

Even one near death desiring to learn, Should be treasured by others. For he is like the empty tea cup, His heart and mind is always open and able to receive.

verse 135-

Take a king and a wise man. These two are not alike. A king is respected in his own country, While a wise man is respected everywhere.

verse 136-

Although the wise man has faults, Philosophers will not grieve over this. Like the moon that shines in its radiance, It is view with pleasure regardless of its stains.

verse 137-

The ego attains great pleasure in accomplishments. The ego attains great misery in mental worry. Patience is the great protector of the mind. Charity is the great protector of the soul.

verse 138-

Although the holy man may live far away, His virtues act as a messenger and carry far. Through sniffing the fragrance of the flowers, The bees are attracted themselves.

verse 139-

If you are pretending to have virtue, There is no use of your arrogant attitude. Like the cow which has no milk, Even if a bell be attached to it, will not be purchased.

verse 140-

While science knows much, our existence is short. We estimate the length of life but we not know for certain. So, like the swan which separates milk from water, Devote yourself to whatever you undertake.

verse 141-

Although there are many stars shining, And the moon shines brightly too. However when the sun sets it becomes night, If not for the sun, there would be no east or west.

verse 142-

On whatever light shines on, Darkness is chased away. The shining of the sun being supreme, What is there in the shining of the moon?

verse 143-

Like the moon, when full, outshines all the stars. The man who accomplishes one single act thoroughly, Surpasses all others who perform many acts. Be as the moon, for the multitude of stars have not this power.

verse 144-

The growth of moral virtue depends on one's self. The acquisition of property depends on previous merit. Why blame anybody for this? For this is the way of nature.

verse 145-

Moral virtues are obtained by making an effort, And as this effort rests wholly within yourself, To say that others possess moral virtues, Is to see yourself in them.

verse 146-

Of those who understand the meaning of the scriptures, There are many even among the crippled. It is a matter for rejoicing to find the sharp-pointed sword, By which the enemy is conquered.

verse 147-

There are rich men among the poor. There are heroes among the cowards. But the holy man who knows the way, Are the rarest of all.

verse 148-

As there are no pearls to be found among elephants, Or gold to be found growing on a tree. The holy and wise that can point to the way, Are not to be found everywhere.

verse 149-

Real Truth is a virtue to the enlightened. But a harmful thing to those living in darkness. The water of the river is very free from impurity; But, entering the ocean, it becomes undrinkable.

verse 150-

The refined relish in refinement.. Barbarians have no use for refinement Bees are attracted by the fragrance of flowers. The frogs, although living together, are not.

verse 151-

The fame of those with keen discernment and sound judgment, Are known among others with the same traits. For they are as valuables among experts, And heroes in battle.

verse 152-

The swan does not fit in well in the company of hawks. Nor does a horse among the pigs, Nor does a lion among the foxes, Nor the clever man among fools.

verse 153-

Those who are acknowledged by the exulted,
Which upon their heads is placed a wreath, May be
considered vulgar by those, Who are unworthy of
such recognition.

verse 154-

Though possessing it, they don't proclaim it. While
others have it in small measure, Holy men delight in
such moral virtue. How remarkable is such conduct!

verse 155-

The ones possessing total awareness, Are only
known by others of total awareness. For the exact
weight of the earth, Is only known to them.

verse 156-

If people let their virtues speak through their
actions, Even those who do not have virtues will
acquire them. But the one who boast of his virtues,
Even if a wise man, would not be respected.

verse 157-

Where being wise and honest is not respected,
Then why would the wise and honest go? In such a
place as that, What would the wise and honest do?

verse 158-

It is the ignorant that mimic each other, For they are incapable of personal thinking. By imitating each other, They remain in the darkness.

verse 159-

The idiot admires the clever man. For he considers him to be superior. The idiot and the clever man acquire wealth, While the wise goes empty handed.

verse 160-

As the sage passes time with various acts of virtue, He notices not his state of indigence. While this extreme poverty seems suffering, To the sage it is not hardship, it is the joy from within.

verse 161-

One who makes company with many people, Spending his days at the market, And yet chooses not to obtain the virtues of the holy, Then what is his profit in being born?

verse 162-

The way of the wise man is knowledge, The way of the cuckoo is a sweet note, The way of the ascetic is patience, The way of a woman is perversity.

verse 163-

Astronomy itself and doctrinal principles, The Eagle-spell and the repeating of spells, (Of these) the essential meaning should be seized. Do not analyze the sound of the words.

verse 164-

Knowledge that is left in books, Wealth that is taken from others, When the time comes that both are needed, Neither will be there

verse 165-

The teacher of the arts has many accomplishments. But these accomplishments come from earning a living, But the study of the termination of earthly incarnation, Why should that not be the only accomplishment?

verse 166-

With great care and thought be made, Before giving sound advice to a man. For like giving pearls to a monkey. It will soon be cast to the ground

verse 167-

Some spend countless hours preaching, Some attain their desire without speaking. The reed-flower has no fruit, The walnut has both flower and fruit.

verse 168-

The nut of the Kataka tree purifies water, By immersing it into the muddy waters. If not immersed but only mentioned, Does the muddy water become clear?

verse 169-

A man that possesses knowledge of the written word, And yet he does not apply what he has learned, Is like a blind man carrying a lamp during the day, He is still unable to see the road.

verse 170-

Like the moon which waxes and wanes, Shines equally on the holy and the ignorant. While you may attain a little virtue, You may also lose vast accomplishments.

verse 171-

It is far easier to have a clever man for one's enemy, Than to be friends with the unlearned and ignorant. For it is better to have a worthy opponent you know, Then to battle a monkey or a cow.

verse 172-

The clever, the disciplined, The contented and the tellers of truth, It is better for such to die, Than to live in the kingdom of the evil.

verse 173-

What is more deadly, a snake's venom or that of an evil man? An evil man is more venomous than a snake, For the snake's venom may be overcome by drugs. But what can soothe the venom of an evil man?

verse 174-

Although the evil may be benefited by fortune and gain. Yet, even when happy, they still use abusive language. He who is well educated and steadfast is firm. Although poor and penniless, he will not abandon virtue.

verse 175-

The naturally evil man, Is like the beam and balance scales. A little thing sends him up, And a little thing brings him down.

verse 176-

Although smeared with sandalwood, musk and camphor, The natural strong smell of garlic is not driven out. Although one may study very well the many texts,   One does not drive out the natural evil in one's disposition.

verse 177-

As there are no markings on the son of a holy man. There are no markings on the son of a prostitute. But the perversion of the act is evident by the presence, And is the essential characteristic of the bastard.

verse 178-

The word which is uttered is one thing, And different from the thought in the mind. This is the way of the crooked- minded, Who can change his natural disposition?

verse 179-

He firmly with resolve retains his vices, While he continues to discard moral virtues. In retaining vice and discarding virtue, The evil man resembles a strainer.

verse 180-

He who has been falsely accused by an evil man, Loses confidence even in the holy and wise. Like a child's mouth has been scalded by hot milk, He will blow even on cold milk before drinking it.

verse 181-

Seeing the stars' reflection on the lake by night, The swan is disappointed in taking them for lotus shoots, Even when he sees the real lotus shoot by day he will not eat it. When once refuted by a liar, one will doubt even the truthful.

verse 182-

Twice as much as a man, a woman's appetite. Four times as much, her deceitfulness. Six times as much, her shame. Eight times as much, her passion, so it is said.

verse 183-

Not by giving gifts or attention. Not by worship or veneration. Not by constant association. None of these will control a woman.

verse 184-

When he was carried off by the King of the Birds, The White Lotus Serpent God said: He who tells secrets to women, His life is lost there and then.

verse 185-

By committing adultery, they destroy the others faith, In their object of desire and religion, Causing much suffering this creates an obstacle to salvation. Therefore avoid the wife of another man.

verse 186-

If even one written verse of truth, Is given by a Lama to his pupil, The gift given would be supreme. Such a thing is not on earth.

verse 187-

All worldly pleasures should be abandoned, But, if you are unable to abandon them, Then cling to the holy with all your might. As this is the cure for it.

verse 188-

All desires should be abandoned, But if you cannot abandon them, Let your desires be for salvation. As this is the cure for it.

verse 189-

The unhelpful brother is like a stranger, But he who helps, even if he is an outsider, is a brother. Like the body and its diseases which are with us, Solitude is the beneficial medicine of the soul.

verse 190-

If you hold a pot full of water over your head, With persistence and diligence, So it is as with respect, The evil man becomes angry and excited.

verse 191-

Whatever may be agreeable to your mind, Although it is far away, it is too, very near. That which is not kept firmly planted in your mind, Although it may be your side, it is too, very far.

verse 192-

Though we may live in the society of the wicked There is no intimacy like the water and the lotus. The holy may ever live far apart, Yet they rejoice like the moon and the water-lily.

verse 193-

If you desire true friendship, Then avoid the following, Gambling , The lending and borrowing of money, And speaking lustily with women.

verse 194-

When milk flows from the bees, When honey flows from a cow, Then, when a woman is true, The lotus will grow in dry ground.

verse 195-

A man possessed of very little moral merit, Even though he obtains abundance, knows not how to enjoy it, Like a dog on a frozen lake, which, when thirsty Licks the ice with its tongue, receives no satisfaction.

verse 196-

Those who do work in this world, Would not work without profit But beggars and the poor, without its being evident. Have a hundredfold profit in the future.

verse 197-

It is natural that we will all die one day Leaving our wealth behind, give alms. When you die your property is not lost, Realize that giving alms is like the act of a clever miser.

verse 198-

The miserable do not give alms, For they fear they may become impoverish. But wealth is the real danger, Knowing this, the learned man distributes his wealth.

verse 199-

Why not give about half of your food to the beggars? Charity brings rewards back to you 10 fold. While you may not see the immediate rewards, It will be obtained at some time.

verse 200-

Even though you may not see results from your actions, Do not be grieved by this, or feel sorrow. You can still give alms from your possessions. Be dedicated in your resolve to give as it is honorable.

verse 201-

Wealth is devoid of charity and enjoyment. Such an owner of wealth in living in error. Even though it is your property, why not use it, Either in giving it away or to be enjoyed.

verse 202-

You are placed here on earth for action. Your results here go to the beyond. Whatever actions you may do here, The same will certainly be enjoyed there

verse 203-

Be envious not for wealth, rank, beauty, and health.
For these are not to be grieved for. If you desire
these, then practice virtuous action. Like the fruits of a
tree came from one time, a seed.

verse 204-

If you hoard your possessions and do not distribute
them, Then what is the use of having them? Like the
fruits of the Horse-apple tree, While bountiful, what is
its use in hunger?

verse 205-

The pleasure in giving alms which do not harm
others, Is a gift that cannot be carried away by water,
Nor burnt by fire or stolen by thieves, Such
possessions will never be utterly destroyed.

verse 206-

He that does not strive for salvation from Hell,
What will he do once he reaches that place? When no
medicine exist for his disease, What will he do other
than die?

verse 207-

Holy men are seized by the snake of words, which
comes from the pit of savage men. As a means of a
cure from this poison, Drink the medicine of wisdom
and patience.

verse 208-

Although you may kill many during your life, You will not reduce the number of your enemies. But if your own anger be slain, That is to slay the real enemy.

verse 209-

The mighty are not easy to reform, Therefore why exercise patience with them. Those who are disciplined and peaceful in conduct What necessity is there for patience?

verse 210-

If you are merely angry owing to a grudge, Then why not be angry with the anger? Which obviously destroys religious aims, For salvation, one must let go of anger.

verse 211-

He who having seen the excellence of others, Is afflicted by envy or jealously in his own mind, Will not gain even a little of the Truth. Such a being destroys his own merit.

verse 212-

Let all hear this moral maxim, And having heard it keep it well: Whatever is not pleasing to yourself, Do not do that unto others.

verse 213-

In regards to leaving this mortal life, Who is not clever in knowing and speaking about it? But when it comes to practicing what they preach Those who do would be considered wise among the sages.

verse 214-

The conduct of mankind is very surprising! Youth perishes with age and property is unsecured. Life is constantly being stalked by Death. Yet mankind clings to this life, refusing to let go.

verse 215-

He who possesses intellect but is lazy, Will never but held in high esteem. Like a child who writes in the dust, His works never bring lastly benefit.

verse 216-

If people, all of the them, Could only perceive Death on their own heads. Even in food there would be no flavor or pleasure. Not to mention other things.

verse 217-

Death does not wait to ask whether, Your works are completed or not. Therefore do tomorrow's work today, And the evening's work in the morning.

verse 218-

As long as you are healthy and produce a harvest, That is not ruined by the great hail of disease, As long as your intellect is in your work, This is the time for adhering to religious doctrines.

verse 219-

What are strings of pearls to donkeys and cattle? What is delicate food to dogs and pigs? Light to the blind or songs to the deaf? Of what use is religious doctrine to fools?

verse 220-

Strive to have your accomplishments serve others, Rather than have them serve your ego. If ego rules your actions, Then how are morals attained?

verse 221-

Strive not to be a beggar, even if the times demands it. Strive to live that of a glorious ascetic. Be brave, clever, that of high rank. Manly are these traits until you beg.

verse 222-

The first to accomplish a difficult task, Is considered a hero. However, in regards to building a fire, It can even be done by a child.

verse 223-

A sage's son may conveniently die soon, And a king's son may conveniently live for a long time. For the hunter's son life and death are equally unsuitable, For the saint's son equally convenient.

verse 224-

Let that which exists in the beginning, continue to exist, For the purpose of increasing man's understanding of them. Let the elegant classics be expounded and learned, By the man who understands these doctrines.

verse 225-

The words of elegant sayings, Should be collected as a convenience. For the temporary but supreme gift of words, Any price will be paid.

verse 226-

The student of science, the hero, And every beautifully formed woman, Wherever they go, Acquire great fame, there and then.

verse 227-

A scientist and a king, Are not to be compared in any way. The king is esteemed in his own country. The wise man is esteemed wherever he goes.

verse 228-

He may be handsome, youthful, accomplished,
And born of high caste, yet, Like a new born hawk or
owl , Does not look well when removed from his nest.

verse 229-

He who has a body but is ignorant of knowledge,
Even though of good birth, what use is he? In the
world respect comes from knowledge. From lack of
knowledge comes destruction.

verse 230-

If you desire an easy life, give up learning. If you
desire learning, give up ease. How can the man at his
ease acquire knowledge, And how can the earnest
student enjoy ease?

verse 231-

He who is ignorant of knowledge, Will always be in
misery and pain. He who is wise in knowledge, Will
always obtain joy and happiness.

verse 232-

What country is foreign to a sage? Who is hostile to
a pleasant speaker? What load is heavy to a man in
his own home? What distance is long to the
energetic?

verse 233-

Since he who is unselfish, has many friends, The summit of the king of mountains is not too high, The earth's depth of intellect are not too deep, And even when torn apart by the ocean it is not beyond his reach.

verse 234-

The superior man who has learned from only books, And has not studied from many different perspectives, Is like a pregnant girl of loose morals. He does not look well at a gathering.

verse 235-

The one that scorns the teaching of a Lama, Even if only a single letter, Will pass through a hundred incarnations, As a dog and be reborn of low caste.

verse 236-

A single grain of wisdom bestowed upon you, By a Lama as you are the pupil, That is a debt that if paid by you, Cannot be sufficiently paid in full.

verse 237-

He who brings one up, he who teaches the way, He who teaches him science, Who feeds one and gives the gift of fearlessness, These five are declared to be like fathers.

verse 238-

The wife of a king or of a minister, Likewise the wife of a friend, A brother's wife, and one's own mother, These five are be treated like mothers.

verse 239-

Giving advice to a fool, While it may excite him, It is still like giving your pearls, To the dogs and pigs.

verse 240-

The fool is nothing more than an inanimate beast. You should especially avoid them. Like stepping on an unseen thorn, The pain of their words hurts.

verse 241-

When a fool sees another fool, He is overcome with joy. If he sees a learned man, He regards him as a murderer.

verse 242-

The evil are not grateful towards you, For any benefit that is given to them. However even the smallest act towards a holy man, Will give you command of him for life.

verse 243-

The actions of a fool is like a stone thrown into the pond, Quickly will the ripples fade away. The actions of a holy man are like a carving on stone, They may be small but they are permanent.

verse 244-

Even though the evil man may speak sweetly, He is not to be trusted at any moment. Like the peacock that has beautiful plumage, It devours and consumes all in its path.

verse 245-

The evil man and phlegm are really alike. By mildness they are both excited, And require attention but, By roughness they are both dealt with.

verse 246-

These are controlled by beating, An evil man, gold, a drum, A wild horse, and cloth These are not the means for elegant doings.

verse 247-

Association with the evil man is not appropriate, Whether he is pleasant or obnoxious. As with a dog, it's not appropriate, whether you play with him or let him lick you.

verse 248-

Reckless abandonment is worse than a snake. A snake's venom can be cured by drugs, But committing reckless abandonment, Cannot be cured by anything.

verse 249-

The sins of the unruly and undisciplined, Leave
their mark on the temperament. Like stepping into
fresh cow dung, Surely you too will carry the smell
with you.

verse 250-

Even without noticing his father's conduct, The son
imitates him. From the Pecan tree, One does not get
oranges.

verse 251-

If my father, my mother, own my brother, And my
wife copy me and my actions, In whatever sin I
commit, It is as if they had committed it too.

verse 252-

This earth, the mighty ocean, And the mountains
are not a burden, But he who is ungrateful towards
nature, Is indeed a heavy burden to mother earth.

verse 253-

He who stays in the society of those of the Way,
And is full of compassion and love for his enemies.
Although he may be destroyed by them, Wise men
will praise him very much.

verse 254-

In the society of the clever, the disciplined, The contented, and the truthful, Imprisonment is a superior state over, The sovereignty of the unruly.

verse 255-

Immersing into the society of the holy. Associate within the society of the learned. Be among the unselfish. These actions will not cause any regrets.
verse 256-

Perhaps for a very long time you've not perceived the misery, Caused by your sins in this world and in the other world, Strive still to bring your mind into the harmony of the way, So you may live in the divine love of the Way.

verse 257-

Although you may enjoy a thing. Yet, if given in fullness would cause bodily harm, And upsets your health, How could such a thing be right to consume?

verse 258-

That is which is painful but required for profit. Like that of a bitter medicine to be cured. The results attained afterwards, In themselves will be incomparable.

verse 259-

If a learned king can grasp the meaning of these verses, From the beginning, to the middle and to the end, And if he realizes that it is as it is written, He will then be in possession of wisdom.

verse 260-

When the ocean shall be no more. It may be crossed in the middle, so they say. Whether holy men exist or not, We should never abandon the moral codes.

CHAPTER FIVE- A ROSE BY ANY OTHER NAME IS STILL A ROSE

From the book- "The Way of the Tao, Living an Authentic Life"

"The names of things do not matter, only what things are."- **William Shakespeare**

I want to show the timeless nature of the principles of the Tao. How these principles have transcended time, religion and political dogmas. The underlying message has been the same regardless of who the messenger was. This has been true since the dawn of man. Throughout history there has been a writer, a philosopher, a ruler or an artist that demonstrated the essence and principles of the Tao. It doesn't matter what you call it, a rose by any other name is still a rose. This is the Tao.

Epictetus was a Greek Stoic philosopher who lived from 55AD to 135AD. He was born a slave and became one of the most famous philosophers of his time. Epictetus's Stoic teachings parallel the philosophy of the Tao. Stoicism and the Tao are both very deeply rooted in spiritually.

Epictetus believed in obtaining a higher awareness of the innerconnectiveness of mankind to all living things and to the universe. Epictetus is one of the key figures of Stoic philosophy and emphasized that virtue is sufficient for happiness.

The basis of his philosophy is that all external events are determined by fate and are out of our control. But we do have the power to accept whatever happens to us in a calmly manner. However individuals are responsible for their own actions which they can and should control. By self-discipline one can become master of controlling their fate. He also taught how it is our responsibility to care for all human beings. He is very consistent in his teachings about man's connection to one another and to nature. He believed followers of this philosophy would achieve happiness and that the joy of life is in the journey.

Another Stoic philosopher, Marcus Aurelius, who is considered to be the most spiritual ruler of all the emperors of Rome, wrote a book called, "Meditations." It is a book based on the philosophy of service and duty. It describes how to find and preserve equanimity in the midst of conflict by following nature as a source of guidance and inspiration. It's not just a set of beliefs; it is a way of life involving practice and discipline. Constant contemplation and the process of living these beliefs

is the life of a Stoic. Stoicism is a spiritual practice of staying in the present, of staying
attentive to your actions and of self-reflection using logic and reason as a foundation.

What is interesting about contemplation is that in Mysticism, contemplation plays an important part in attaining higher states of consciousness. Through contemplation, one is able to stay on the path. This is a key principle of the Tao, contemplation.

Several of the basic tenets of Stoic philosophy are very similar to the principles of the Tao. Let's take a look at a few of these Stoic tenets. "Live life with ethics, virtue, and honor." "Freedom is secured not by the fulfilling of men's desires, but by the removal of desire." Another one, "Outward things cannot touch the soul, not in the least degree; nor have any admission to the soul, nor can they turn or move the soul; but the soul turns and move's itself alone." And lastly, "Virtue is nothing else than right reason, pursue it to the hilt."

The Tao can be found in Jewish Mysticism. In the Zohar, one of the texts of Jewish Mysticism one can find references to the Tao. Jewish Mysticism deals with the "Law" which is very similar to the Tao. Their belief is if one can be one with the Law, then his eternal salvation is assured by being in that oneness. The paradox of this belief is by being in a state of oneness; you are already in a state of eternity.

Within the Zohar, concerning spiritual progression in the here and hereafter, the Zohar states that the soul of a man who has consecrated himself to the study of the Law will upon leaving his earthly body go to a blissful abode by the pathways of the Law, so that his knowledge acquired on earth is of use to him in the hereafter, but those who have willfully neglected to obtain knowledge go astray along roads that lead to "Geburah," a state of suffering. Symbolically speaking the Law acting as the guardian and protector goes before the soul which has delighted itself in sacred study and opens all celestial doors before it. The Law clears the path for the soul to follow and the Law remains with the soul until the day of resurrection when it will serve as the soul's defender.

The Mystic Jews call it the law, the Christians call it God, the Pagans call it several different names but in the end, they are all describing the same thing, a divine consciousness. Once you learn the essence of the Tao, you'll begin to see it in everything and everywhere.

Ralph Waldo Emerson is an excellent example of someone that lived in harmony with nature and with the Tao. Throughout his life he demonstrated time and time again living within the Tao. He was often referred to as the "Concord Sage" during his lifetime and for good reason. These Taoist tendencies are very noticeable in his writings. An example of this can be found in his essay, "The Oversoul," first published in 1841. Here is an excerpt from his essay,

"We live in succession, in division, in parts, in particles. Meantime within man is the soul of the whole; the wise silence; the universal beauty, to which every part and particle is equally related, the eternal ONE. And this deep power in which we exist and whose beatitude is all accessible to us, is not only self-sufficing and perfect in every hour, but the act of seeing and the thing seen, the seer and the spectacle, the subject and the object, are one. We see the world piece by piece, as the sun, the moon, the animal, the tree; but the whole, of which these are shining parts, is the soul."

Here we see his thoughts on the oneness of the universe, the innerconnectiveness of nature, the power of silence and living as a whole in a dualistic world of which are all contained in the Tao.

As a leading philosopher of the transcendentalist movement during the 1800's Emerson brought forth ideas on creative intuition, self-reliance, and the individual's own unlimited potential. He was instrumental in bringing awareness and enlightenment to his fellow men. He believed that by transcending the limits of rationalism and the perceived tradition of his time, one could fully realize their potential.

His views which were the basis of transcendentalism suggested that God does not have to reveal the truth because the truth could be experienced intuitively directly from nature. His beliefs were all things are connected to God and, therefore, all things are divine. As you can imagine his religious views were often considered radical among the religious leaders of his time. However his views and beliefs are very reminiscent of the way of the Tao.

One of the most compelling pieces that Emerson wrote concerning the importance of the connection with nature was from one of his early lectures that became the foundation for his first published work known as the essay, "Nature." Here is an excerpt from that 1836 essay,

"Nature is a language and every new fact one learns is a new word; but it is not a language taken to pieces and dead in the dictionary, but the language put together into a most significant and universal sense. I wish to learn this language, not that I may know a new grammar, but that I may read the great book that is written in that tongue."

Emerson knew the way of the Tao and the power contained within nature. Whether he knew of the Tao or not, I don't know but it is evident by his work and his life that he was definitely living the principles of the Tao.

An interesting facet of Emerson's personal relationship with nature was shared by his son, Doctor Edward Emerson, some years later after his father's death. The Doctor was asked about his father's method of writing. His reply is quite insightful and remarkable into the power of his father's connection with nature. He said,

"It was my father's custom to go daily to the woods to listen. He would remain there an hour or more in order to get whatever there might be there for him that day. He would then come home and write into a little book, his "day-book," of what he had gotten. Later on, when it came time to write a book, he would transcribe from this, in their proper sequence and with their proper connections, these entrances of the preceding weeks or months. The completed book became virtually a ledger formed or posted from his day-books."

It seems that Emerson had found the very heart and soul of God, of the Tao within nature while being in those woods. I would venture to say that Emerson had found a way to listen to the divine in the silence. In those moments, he was one with nature, connected with the Tao. It was the knowledge and wisdom of the Tao that allowed him to communicate with the divine. This is an excellent example of living in the essence of nature.

Another example would be the works of John Burroughs, an American naturalist who was important in the evolution of the conservation movement in America. Burroughs was heavily influenced by the works of Ralph Waldo Emerson and equally influenced by his love of nature. His biographer, Edward Renehan said that Burroughs was a literary naturalist with the duty to record his own unique perceptions of the nature world. To illustrate his views of nature I submit this passage from, "The Summit of the Years" which was published in 1913.

"I am in love with this world; by my constitution I have nestled lovingly in it. It has been home to me. It has been my point of outlook into the universe. I have not bruised myself against it, nor tried to use it ignobly. I have tilled its soil. I have gathered its harvests, I have waited upon its seasons and always have I reaped what I have sown. While I gathered its bread and meat for my body, I did not neglect to gather its bread and meat for my soul."

Another excerpt that shows his sense of wonderment and reverence for nature is from the essay, "The Heart of the Southern Catskills," published in the late 1880's.

"The works of man dwindle, and the original features of the huge globe come out. Every single object or point is dwarfed; the valley of the Hudson is only a wrinkle in the earth's surface. You discover with a

feeling of surprise that the great thing is the earth itself, which stretches away on every hand so far beyond your ken."

In reading the writings of John Burroughs you see a profound spirituality in his views of nature. For Burroughs to have such a deep and profound respect and love for nature, he must have had that connection of oneness that the Tao speaks of. While John Burroughs might have not known of the Tao, his writings say otherwise.

Herman Melville is best known for his novel, "Moby Dick" which is considered to be one of the most important American literary masterpieces of the twentieth century. He was very spiritual and had a keen insight into the connection between the nature of man and the nature of nature. It is evident in his writings such as his belief that the one and only voice of God is silence. Here is one of his comments about nature and the innerconnectiveness of man,

"We cannot live only for ourselves. A thousand fibers connect us with our fellow men; and among those fibers, as sympathetic threads, our actions run as causes, and they come back to us as effects."

This is a very fair representation of the principle of the inner-connectiveness of nature as in the Tao. Melville's understanding of nature and man are based in the Tao and again, I doubt he knew of the Tao.

Another snapshot into the soul of Melville can be seen in this excerpt from a letter he wrote to Nathaniel Hawthorne in the summer of 1851,

"We shall sit down in Paradise in some little shady corner by ourselves; and if we shall by any means be able to smuggle a basket of champagne and if we shall cross our celestial legs in the celestial grass that is forever tropical, and strike our glasses and our heads together till both ring musically in concert: then, O my dear fellow mortal, how shall we pleasantly discourse of all the things manifold which now so much distress us."

While this illustrates Melville's mood of serene desolation at the time, it's a skeptically humorous outlook at man's vanity of gloating over frivolous victories that are worthless outside this domain. It is as if he is laughing at the absurdity of man. He is quoted as saying as much, *"Whatever my fate, I'll go to it laughing."*

At the time he wrote this letter he was only 32 years old and had already lived more life than most men could only dream of. He also had achieved literary success and fame. But in it all he seemed to realize that life was nothing more than an exercise of experiencing being a human. He knew there was more to life and had discovered in his adventures the key to what that more was. He had a distinct connection and love for nature along with an understanding of the illusion of this world. This can be seen in this quote from Moby Dick,

"Me thinks we have hugely mistaken this matter of Life and Death. Me thinks that what they call my shadow here on earth is my true substance. Me thinks that in looking at things spiritual, we are too much like oysters observing the sun through the water, and thinking that thick water the thinnest of air. Me thinks my body is but the lees of my better being. In fact take my body who will, take it I say, it is not me."

Melville's views on obtaining happiness and meaning should not be in the pursuit of some mythical in the sky religious account of the order of things but rather through our actions and relationships with one another and with nature. He believed the meanings one derives from being dedicated to "The wife, the heart, the bed, the table, the saddle, the fire-side, the community, the country," are the genuine meanings of life. The acquiring of these meanings are enough to overcome any threat on the eternal life and by these meanings one's life will not dissolve into a series of meaningless events. When an individual commits to living a life of meaning it is deserving of admiration even if it doesn't fit the tradition of Christianity.

Melville's approach seems to recognize that the presence of the many distinct and good ways of life was something that could and should be strived for. He felt that it would be highly beneficial for a person to search and attain these meanings. In other words, live a virtuous life with respect for one another. While these beliefs are similar to Stoic philosophy and the Tao, I believe it is relevant to point out that the Tao can be disguised in many forms. In using Melville's own words to prove the point,

"Truth is in things, and not in words."

George Carlin! Yes, I said George Carlin. I didn't throw this in just to see if you are paying attention. Nope, George Carlin is part of this group too. Part of understanding the Tao is realizing the reality of the illusion that we are living in. "Getting it" is a big part of the Tao and George Carlin got it. He offered his perspective of how he viewed the world in the form of comedy.

In a way he was our generations' version of Mark Twain. I believe in less than fifty years from now his comedy routines will be taught in philosophy classes in universities throughout America. His Taoist nature was to show us the absurdity of our actions but he failed in believing that we would see the truth hidden in his humor. Given time, some of us have figured it out and now realize what a treasure we had in him.

Carlin had a side to him that has been forgotten that offers an insight into his connection with the Tao. I want you to think about these comments. I want you to see his soul. It is important for you to learn not to dismiss someone because they don't fit the guidelines of what is acceptable. Sometimes it is these people that are on the outside of society that have the best view. Here are a few of his views through his axioms:

1-Throw out non-essential numbers. This includes age, weight and height. Let the doctors worry about them. That is why you pay them.

2- Keep only cheerful friends. The grouches pull you down.

3- Keep learning! Learn more about the computer, crafts, gardening, whatever, even ham radio.

4- Never let the brain idle. "An idle mind is the devil's workshop." And the devil's family name is Alzheimer's.

5- Enjoy the simple things. Laugh often, long, and loud. Laugh until you gasp for breath.

6- The tears happen. Endure, grieve, and move on. The only person who is with us our entire life is ourselves. Be ALIVE while you are alive.

7- Surround yourself with what you love, whether it's family, pets, keepsakes, music, plants, hobbies, whatever. Your home is your refuge.

8- Cherish your health. If it is good, preserve it. If it is unstable, improve it. If it is beyond what you can improve, get help.

9- Don't take guilt trips. Take a trip to the mall, even to the next county; to a foreign country but NOT to where the guilt is.

10- Tell the people you love that you love them at every opportunity.

11- Capitalism tries for a delicate balance: It attempts to work things out so that everyone gets just enough stuff to keep them from getting violent and trying to take other people's stuff.

12- I'm having fun because I don't take life seriously - the only things I care about are my family, friends, work and my lady, Sally. Philosophers for a long time have said 'Why are we here?' - I'm here for the entertainment. If you're born in the world, you're given a ticket to the freak show; if you're born in America, you get a front row seat.

And one more from George,

"Life is not measured by the number of breaths we take, but by the moments that take our breath away. And if you don't send this to at least 8 people - who cares? But do share this with someone. We all need to live life to its fullest each day!"

There is so much we can learn from all these people about life if we would only take the time to look and listen. To borrow from George; we all need to learn to live life to its fullest every day!

CHAPTER SIX- NATIVE AMERICANS AND THE UNIVERSAL NATURE OF THE TAO

From the book- "The Way of the Tao, Living an Authentic Life"

There have been groups of people throughout history who have lived in the way of the Tao. The Native Americans are a great example of a group who strived to live in the way of the Tao. This shows the universal nature of the Tao of how when people live in accordance with the laws of nature, they naturally move towards living a more authentic life.

One only needs to look at the beliefs of the Native Americans to see the evidence of their profound respect of nature. The Native Americans would only kill animals for food or in defense, never for sport. They would never cut down a living tree for firewood unless there were no other options. They had respect for all living things because they knew the innerconnectiveness of the universal consciousness.

They considered themselves caretakers of their domain. They never saw themselves as owners with the right to do whatever they felt like doing. They maintained their respect for nature, which was first and foremost in their lives. They considered themselves responsible for how they leave the land for at least the next 7 generations. In the western world, I doubt most people think about they are doing next year much less what kind of legacy we are leaving for our grandchildren's grandchildren.

The Native Americans have an understanding of the innerconnectiveness of life and nature. It is engrained into their belief system. For a group of people with no organized structure or resemblance to the Western world, they seem to have a deep profound knowledge of the mysteries of life.

They lived in peace and harmony not only with their fellow man but with nature. Black Elk is quoted for saying this about peace,

"The first peace, which is the most important, is that which comes within the souls of people when they realize their relationship, their oneness with the universe and all its powers, and when they realize that at the center of the universe dwells the Great Spirit, and that this center is really everywhere, it is within each of us."

People who are in the Tao are called Sage's. It is important to know what a Sage sounds like when he speaks. One of the most famous Native American

Sages was Chief Seattle. There is a speech that is reported to have been given by Chief Seattle in 1854. It was in response to a proposed treaty which the Indians were persuaded to sell two million acres of land for $150,000.

I first heard the speech in 1988 when it was recited by Joseph Campbell. Campbell was an American writer best known for his work in comparative mythology and religion, author of several books including "The Power of Myth." His philosophy is often summarized by his famous quote, "Follow your bliss."

At the time I heard this speech I was moved by the eloquence, insight and depth of the words. It was beautiful and profound in the way these thoughts were expressed with such vividness. It wasn't until I discovered the Tao that I realized how similar these two philosophies were. It was at this time I realized that the Tao is most definitely universal. This was a moment of clarity into the meaning and nature of the Tao.

Following is the text of Chief Seattle's famous speech. This provides an excellent example of how a Sage communicates with his fellow man. See if these words have an effect on your soul.

"How can you buy or sell the sky, the warmth of the land? The idea is strange to us.

If we do not own the freshness of the air and the sparkle of the water, how can you buy them?

Every part of this earth is sacred to my people. Every shining pine needle, every sandy shore, every mist in the dark woods, every clearing and humming insect is holy in the memory and experience of my people. The sap which courses through the trees carries the memories of the red man.

The white man's dead forget the country of their birth when they go to walk among the stars. Our dead never forget this beautiful earth, for it is the mother of the red man. We are part of the earth and it is part of us. The perfumed flowers are our sisters; the deer, the horse, the great eagle, these are our brothers. The rocky crests, the juices in the meadows, the body heat of the pony, and man --- all belong to the same family.

So, when the Great Chief in Washington sends word that he wishes to buy our land, he asks much of us. The Great Chief sends word he will reserve us a place so that we can live comfortably to ourselves. He will be our father and we will be his children.

So, we will consider your offer to buy our land. But it will not be easy. For this land is sacred to us. This shining water that moves in the streams and rivers is not just water but the blood of our ancestors. If we sell you the land, you must remember that it is sacred, and you must teach your children that it is sacred and that each ghostly reflection in the clear water of the lakes tells of events and memories in the life of my people. The water's murmur is the voice of my father's father.

The rivers are our brothers, they quench our thirst. The rivers carry our canoes, and feed our children. If we sell you our land, you must remember, and teach your children, that the rivers are our brothers and yours, and you must henceforth give the rivers the kindness you would give any brother.

We know that the white man does not understand our ways. One portion of land is the same to him as the next, for he is a stranger who comes in the night and takes from the land whatever he needs. The earth is not his brother, but his enemy, and when he has conquered it, he moves on. He leaves his father's grave behind, and he does not care. He kidnaps the earth from his children, and he does not care. His father's grave, and his children's birthright are forgotten. He treats his mother, the earth, and his brother, the sky, as things to be bought, plundered, sold like sheep or bright beads. His appetite will devour the earth and leave behind only a desert.

I do not know. Our ways are different than your ways. The sight of your cities pains the eyes of the red man. There is no quiet place in the white man's cities. No place to hear the unfurling of leaves in spring or the rustle of the insect's wings. The clatter only seems to insult the ears.

And what is there to life if a man cannot hear the lonely cry of the whippoorwill or the arguments of the frogs around the pond at night? I am a red man and do not understand. The Indian prefers the soft sound of the wind darting over the face of a pond and the smell of the wind itself, cleaned by a midday rain, or scented with pinon pine.

The air is precious to the red man for all things share the same breath, the beast, the tree, the man; they all share the same breath. The white man does not seem to notice the air he breathes. Like a man dying for many days he is numb to the stench. But if we sell you our land, you must remember that the air is precious to us, that the air shares its spirit with all the life it supports.

The wind that gave our grandfather his first breath also receives his last sigh. And if we sell you our land, you must keep it apart and sacred as a place where even the white man can go to taste the wind that is sweetened by the meadow's flowers.

So we will consider your offer to buy our land. If we decide to accept, I will make one condition - the white man must treat the beasts of this land as his brothers.

I am a savage and do not understand any other way. I have seen a thousand rotting buffaloes on the prairie, left by the white man who shot them from a passing train. I am a savage and do not understand how the smoking iron horse can be made more important than the buffalo that we kill only to stay alive.

What is man without the beasts? If all the beasts were gone, man would die from a great loneliness of the spirit. For whatever happens to the beasts, soon happens to man. All things are connected.

You must teach your children that the ground beneath their feet is the ashes of our grandfathers. So that they will respect the land, tell your children that the earth is rich with the lives of our kin. Teach your children that we have taught our children that the earth is our mother. Whatever befalls the earth befalls the sons of earth. If men spit upon the ground, they spit upon themselves.

This we know; the earth does not belong to man; man belongs to the earth. This we know. All things are connected like the blood which unites one family. All things are connected.

Even the white man, whose God walks and talks with him as friend to friend, cannot be exempt from the common destiny. We may be brothers after all. We shall see. One thing we know which the white man may one day discover; our God is the same God.

You may think now that you own Him as you wish to own our land; but you cannot. He is the God of man, and His compassion is equal for the red man and the white. The earth is precious to Him, and to harm the earth is to heap contempt on its creator. The whites too shall pass; perhaps sooner than all other tribes. Contaminate your bed and you will one night suffocate in your own waste.

But in your perishing you will shine brightly fired by the strength of the God who brought you to this land and for some special purpose gave you dominion over this land and over the red man.

That destiny is a mystery to us, for we do not understand when the buffalo are all slaughtered, the wild horses are tamed, the secret corners of the forest heavy with the scent of many men and the view of the ripe hills blotted by talking wires.

This is the end of living and the beginning of survival."

Last of these examples of the native people living the principles of the Tao is by Chief White Cloud. I want to share a little wisdom from this great Sage.

"Your religious calling was on plates of stone by the flaming finger of an angry God.

Our religion was established by the traditions of our ancestors, the dreams of our elders that are given to them in the silent hours of the night by the Great Spirit, and by the premonitions of the learned Beings.

It is written in the hearts of our people, thus: We do not require churches which would only lead to us to argue about GOD. We do not wish this. Earthy things may be argued about by men, but we never argue over GOD.

And the thought that white men should rule over nature and change its ways following his liking was never understood by the Red man.

Our belief is that the Great Spirit has created all things. Not just mankind, but all animals, all plants, all rocks... For us all, life is holy. But you do not understand our prayers when we address the sun, moon, and winds. You have judged us without understanding, only because our prayers are different. But we are able to live in harmony with all of nature.

All of nature is within us and we are part of all nature."

CHAPTER SEVEN- ZEN AND BAMBOO

From the book- "Hsin Hsin Ming"

In trying to describe Zen, it is easier to say what it isn't. Zen isn't a religion. A religion is dualistic. Religion has a good god and an evil devil. Within religion there is a choice to make, to either be on the side of good or on the side of evil. Zen doesn't take sides.

Zen isn't a philosophy. Philosophy is a commentary of a particular view on a subject. Philosophy is one-sided derived from judgment. It is man-made, it is the study of issues and problems with an attempt to find answers. Philosophy is very logical, very systematic, very rational. Zen isn't man-made.

Zen is a fusion of Buddhism and Taoism. It is the teachings of Buddha combined with the teachings of Lao Tzu. The roots of Zen are very deep in these two schools. The foundation of Zen is firmly planted on these two schools of thought.

Zen is unaffected by the changing times, whether it is political or otherwise. Zen is timeless. Nothing can change it, it is eternity within itself. It is the one constant in this world. Ever unchanging. It teaches to be in this world but not of this world. You are here so be here in this world.

This might seem a bit of a contradiction. The meaning here is to be in the world and immerse yourself into it, but do not become attach to it. Don't let anything cling to you that will bring pain when it is removed. That doesn't mean not to love or to hole up in a cave. No, it means to have the enlightenment that there is no lost, only change. How can a loved one go anywhere, there is nowhere to go, there is only now.

Being unaffected by things is to be free from the attachment of the illusions of this world. A way to illustrate this illusionary state is through a TV. When you are watching a TV program, say like Brian Greene's "Fabric of the Cosmos," Are you really seeing Brian Greene? The answer is No! In reality what you are seeing is thousands upon thousands of little dots of different colors. Freeze the program on the TV, take a magnifying glass and look at the screen, what will you see? Nothing but thousands of these dots. These dots are not Brian Greene, there are dots! Just dots! Some are red, some are yellow, some are blue and some are black. So, just exactly what are you looking at? A matrix of strategically placed dots to create the illusion of Brian Greene. Nothing more. If you were to blow up the image a

1,000 times, there would no evidence of anything other than dots. It isn't any different with life. Science has shown that anything taken down to the sub-atomic level shows nothing more than mostly empty space, like the image on the TV screen, there really isn't anything there.

On attachment, treat life the way you watch a movie. When you go to the movies, you suspend your logic and sense of belief for those few hours. During the movie, you laugh, you cry, you feel and connect to the characters and their lives there on the screen. However, once the movie is finished, you get up and leave the theater. You leave the experience behind. You do not run up to the screen and try to peel the character off the screen so you may possess it and take it home nor do you grieve for the movie ending. It's just a movie. You know that whenever you want to experience those feelings, you simply watch the movie again.

It is the same with this life. Immerse yourself into life and enjoy it to the fullest, after all, that is why you are here. Become rooted and grounded into this world. But remember not to let attachments, judgments, or opinions cloud your nature. Be unchanging in your inner true self, your Buddha-nature. Yielding but unchanging. Live in the now for that is where eternity resides.

Overcome duality to discover your Buddha-nature. See pass the obstacles of movement and rest. Be of one mind. One-mind is considered in a meditative context to be free of duality. When the mind is free from things and free from attachments, it can function in this world and still be uninfluenced by the actions of the world. Once the attachments have been removed, the true substance can be revealed to you. To live in this faith is to be free from duality while living in a dualistic world.

To live a true life, is to have no need to make waves on the ocean when there is no wind. For this is the way of a Zen Master.

So, what does this have to do with Bamboo? Bamboo is considered a symbol of Zen. It is a tree that has great roots firmly planted into the soil. Strength comes from its strong roots. It is this strength of being so grounded into the soil that allows it to be yielding when confronted with adversarial winds and storms.

It is always green, in winter, spring, summer or fall, always green, always full of life, always growing, always unchanging. Bamboo is empty inside, clinging to nothing in this world other than the substance needed to support its life. It's soul isn't cluttered with senseless desires or opinions. It remains empty, one with the nothingness. Yes, bamboo makes for an excellent symbol for Zen.

CHAPTER EIGHT- ON MEANING NOTHINGNESS AND ENLIGHTENMENT

From the book, "Hsin Hsin Ming"

Throughout Buddhism, Taoism and Zen there it much talk and mention about Nothingness, Emptiness, Oneness, the Void, and Suchness. In the western world, this makes no sense, "There has to be something, even nothing is something, right?" The western world cannot understand these meanings, maybe because there are no meaning to these words in the East. This is a major conflict between the two worlds. The west always believes that there is meaning in everything, there is always a "why" and a meaning to that "why." In Zen, in the true meaning of life, there is no meaning. In Zen, it is call existence. In existence, there is no need for a meaning or explanation, it just is what it is.

There is a story about Picasso the painter. One day an observer watched Picasso start a painting. As the day wore on Picasso continued to paint till he finished with the work in the afternoon. Upon completion, the observer asked Picasso what the painting represented, what was the meaning of it. Picasso became upset, angry, even mad. He shouted, "Go ask the roses in the garden what is the meaning of the roses! Why do people come to me and ask for the meaning? If the rose can be there without any meaning, then why cannot my painting be there without any meaning?"

Meanings are a thing of the mind. It is the mind that seeks a meaning to everything. Sometimes this is a good thing, like in science and medicine. But for nature, there is no meaning, there is just is. This is the precept of existence in nature, for there is no need for meaning. Look at it this way, how absurd would it be to ask a cloud, "What is the meaning of this? Why are you here and where did you come from?" I am sure the cloud will have no answer for you. Because the cloud is being a cloud, doing what clouds do. That is the dharma of a cloud and it is fulfilling that dharma. It would be the same thing if you asked a dog why it barks. What do you think the answer would be? The dog cannot answer the question, because it doesn't understand why you're asking such a question. Dogs bark and cats meow, because that is their nature.

If a sentient being is living its dharma, there is no need for meaning, its existence is enough. All throughout nature, there isn't any meaning placed on anything by nature. It is us that has a ego driven need for meaning and to place meaning on things. If we do not have meaning we began to feel insecure and worried. We feel out of place or disconnected. This behavior isn't seen in nature, only in man.

In creating meaning, we create separation. As long we are in separation, there can be no enlightenment. Enlightenment is losing separation and meaning. When you focus on the meaning of something, you have missed the point. Because the something really isn't what it appears to be.

On the subject of Nothingness being the primary objective of Zen. Brian Greene, the noted Physicist from Colombia University wrote a great book called, "The Fabric of the Cosmos." The book has also been made into a TV series shown on PBS. In his book, there is a section on, "What is Space." This is where I will show you that science is catching up to Eastern Thought on nothingness. To quote Brian Greene from the show on "What is Space,"

"We think of our world as filled with stuff, like buildings and cars, buses and people. And nowhere does that seem more apparent than in a crowded city like New York.

Yet all around the stuff that makes up our everyday world is something just as important but far more mysterious: the space in which all this stuff exists.

To get a feel for what I'm talking about, let's stop for a moment and imagine. What if you took all this stuff away? I mean all of it: the people, the cars and buildings. And not just the stuff here on Earth, but the earth itself; what if you took away all the planets, stars and galaxies? And not just the big stuff, but tiny things down to the very last atoms of gas and dust; what if you took it all away? What would be left?

Most of us would say "nothing." And we'd be right. But strangely, we'd also be wrong. What's left is empty space. And as it turns out, empty space is not nothing. It's something, something with hidden characteristics as real as all the stuff in our everyday lives.

In fact, space is so real it can bend, space can twist, and it can ripple; so real that empty space itself helps shape everything in the world around us and forms the very fabric of the cosmos."

What Brian Greene is talking about here is that science is discovering that there is a "Mysterious Force" out in space, out in this nothingness, in this emptiness, and in the void, that is controlling our world. This force is more powerful than we can imagine. Our world, our galaxy, our universe is mostly empty space, and it is this "space" that dictates what happens here.

According to Brian, it seems that we actually live in a illusionary world, a sort of a matrix. The illusionary aspects are really driven home in this next quote from Brian Greene,

"In fact, if you removed all the space inside all the atoms making up the stone, glass and steel of the

Empire State building, you would be left with a little lump, about the size of a grain of rice but weighing hundreds of millions of pounds. The rest is only empty space."

So maybe this is the meaning of nothingness in Zen, the knowing that all we see, feel and touch is nothing more than an illusion. There must be a way to attain freedom from this illusion and get out of the "stuff," and the "matrix," and see the true reality, the true reality that cannot be seen while still living in and under this illusion.

Science is telling us now that it is what we don't see or know that is the real factor in determining our fates as a species. Could it be that different from Eastern Thought? Within this mysterious emptiness, nothingness could be a whole another world where duality does not exist and the truth lives. There is something powerful out there and Zen knows what it is.

Enlightenment is like this, it is not in attaining truths, it is about removing lies. Lies that have manifested in false beliefs. Once all the lies have been removed, there is nothing but space, complete emptiness, complete nothingness, that is where the real truth resides.

By removing choices, judgments, and separateness, by not trying to put meaning to everything, but to just reflect life, to become like the cloud, to search for nothing knowing that there is nothing to find, maybe this is the way to break free from the grain of rice and see the reality that the illusion is hiding from us. It is the clinging to false beliefs that has trapped us in this matrix. This is the purpose of Zen, to remove yourself from it and return to your true nature. To return to your true nature in this world, learn to use your mind and yet be free from any attachment. The true nature is unborn therefore undying, it neither moves or stays, it is already complete, and all that is needed is already here. Learn this principle.

An example of this is illustrated in this little story about when Hui Neng, the sixth and last patriarch of Chan, lied dying. One of the students there with him by his bedside asked, "Master, where are you going?" This question must be in reference as to where Hui Neng's soul would go upon death. Hui Neng replied, " What a foolish question? Where can one go? There is nowhere to go. One is always here, now."

What Hui Neng is saying that you are always here. There is no then or here then there. There is only now. That what has gone is gone and you can no more go to yesterday than you can go to tomorrow because you can only be here now. When tomorrow does come, then it is here now, it is always here now. There is no way you can be anywhere else. So therefore there isn't any place to go to and nobody to go anywhere. You are all with everything already, there is no fear of death, no dread nor no nirvana to achieve. Only now. There is nothing to be done, nothing to cling to, only just be. When a world comes to an end, another begins. Just like there was a yesterday, there will be a tomorrow, but till then there is only now so be here in this now, the yesterdays and tomorrows will take care of themselves in their own accord.

So live life and be aware of all that surrounds you. Learn to listen to the sound of the running water of a stream, or the sounds of the songbirds, become silent and quiet and learn to listen with your soul. Close your eyes and imagine that you are that waterfall or the songbird, feel the breeze has it blows through the tress and across the grass. Learn to listen to the connectiveness of it all. Learn to hear what isn't being said, learn to hear with your soul and true self. In the silence and quietness, you'll rediscover your Buddha-nature, your true authentic self, and experience what Seng-Ts'an is conveying in the Hsin Hsin Ming. Use the Hsin Hsin Ming as a guide to enlightenment.

"A true life has no need to raise waves when the wind is not blowing."

In seeking, you'll never find it. The very act of seeking creates separation. As long as separation exist, attainment cannot be had. Cease to seek and separation vanishes. Cease to seek to become whole.

Enlightenment- All enlightenment is sudden. The real question is how long does it take to get there. On these instances of sudden enlightenment, it usually happens in a moment of crystal clarity. These moments are also called having an epiphany. All of us have had at one time or another one of these moments of a major break-through. Some of us call it a light bulb moment when the light comes on when we have that "ah, now I get it" moment. If you were to recall one of those moments, you'll see that you were more than likely in a state of deep contemplation. It is when you are in these intense deep states of contemplation that profound answers are reveled to you. It doesn't matter if it is a math problem or trying to solve a serious issue within your life, the answers always seem to appear during these states of intense deep contemplation.

A way to explain sudden enlightenment is to imagine yourself in a dark room groping for the light switch. Some people find the light switch rather quickly while others spend countless hours in search of the light switch. And there are those who are content to just sit in the middle of the room and do nothing. This is true of searching for enlightenment. It is through contemplation that one finds the answers.

Imagine that contemplation is the process of doubt. The doubt being that it doesn't have to be this way and no other. It is the doubt that drives you to find that other way. The greater the doubt, the greater the resolve in finding what it is that you are looking for. The lesser the doubt, the lesser the commitment will be and if there is no doubt, then no movement or desire to look.

If you doubt or refuse to accept the darkness, and have great desire, as great as your doubt that things do not have to stay this way, you're going to do something about it and start looking for that switch. No matter how intense your resolve is to find the switch, once found and turned on, the light appears in an instance.

However, if you are content with the darkness and accept it, then there is no doubt in your life, because you accept It. Therefore, you have no desire or motivation to do anything about it. You will continue to sit there in the dark till the end of time. Even worst, is if you take no action because you believe that there is no other way of living besides living in the dark. Either way, you are confined to the darkness until you have a change of state within your mind. You are stuck because you do not doubt the situation nor do you contemplate on how to change it.

Within Ch'an and Zen, contemplation is the art of taking dead words and bringing life to them. It is through contemplation that you begin to place yourself into the question and strive to understand what it is that you are to learn. This is where doubt plays a major role. By doubting that you think you understand, you look for other answers and meanings. At first the statement or question seems to be confusing. For example, the gong'an, " One day a monk asked Master Zhaozhou, "Does a dog have Buddha-nature or not." Zhaozhou replied," No!"

It is known in Buddhist teachings that all sentient beings have Buddha-nature, even dogs. So what is the point that Zhaozhou is making here? From the onset you know this statement makes no sense. You doubt that Zhaozhou meant for us to take this statement at face value, you know there has to be more to it but what? Through contemplation, creating doubt and questioning, you are able to break through the doubt and reach oneness. It is in this state of no-mind where there is no-self that the statement makes sense. This process is done without thinking as much as it is done through immersion by reflection. Even Rene Descartes said, "if you would be a seeker after the truth, it is necessary that at least once in your life you doubt, as far as possible; all things. Break free and live life on your own terms. Think for yourself."

It is with the practice of great doubt in contemplation that you see the real question that the monk asked. In reality, by the monk asking the question, it demonstrated that he, the monk, did not have presence of Buddha-nature. In reality, the monk was asking if he had Buddha-nature. If he had awareness of his own Buddha-nature, he wouldn't have asked the question. Therefore, the answer was "No!" You got to believe it before you know it and if you don't believe it, then it isn't so.

Like being in that dark room, if you do not believe that there is a light switch that can illuminate the room for you, then there is no light switch in your reality. So why would you ask if there is a light switch in the other room for someone else? This is the point to the answer.

If you are in that dark room and refuse to believe that there is nothing more than the darkness, then you have created doubt. When you create doubt, you must believe that there must be more to what you see. With this doubt, you enter into a state of contemplation. It is this state that drives you to feel along the walls for that switch, searching for an answer, even if you are unsure just exactly what that answer is. On finding the switch, illumination comes in an instance, it doesn't matter how long the journey might have been to get to that point, enlightenment comes in an instance. In that instance, all within the room is revealed to you and in addition, the door from which to leave!

The key to enlightenment then is contemplation. It is an universal concept, whether it is Jewish or Christian Mysticism, Eastern or Western faiths. Contemplation is a central point in all spiritual traditions. In the west it might be called prayer, in the east it is referred to as mediation, whatever you want to call it, it is the primary path to enlightenment.

So, what does life look like when someone has attain enlightenment. According to an old Buddhism proverb, "The unenlightened chop wood and carry water. When one becomes enlightened, he chops wood and carries water." I have been asked several times what this means as it makes no sense to most people in the beginning. Most people believe that upon enlightenment something mysterious happens and you attain some special power. Well, in a way you do, but not in the way most people think. The power is in the heighten state of awareness that you have. It is in the ability to see what is in front of you that others cannot see. I want to answer the question with this quote about something as simple as building a fire in the fireplace at home during the winter to keep warm. You'll see what I mean by having awareness attain through enlightenment. This quote sums it up rather well, let me know what you think,

"Upon returning home on a cold winter night, I begin my evening by building a fire in the fireplace to chase away the chill. Once I have gather the logs and placed them so, I start the fire. At the birth of the flames starting to flicker among the logs, it is in that moment I know that I am releasing all the memories that have been stored up in that tree. I know that I am releasing the sunshine that gave warmth to that tree , that tree from whence the firewood came. I know that I am releasing the clouds that gave it shade, the rain that quench its thirst, the soil from which it received its nourishment, and all those enjoyments that the tree experienced so joyfully, like those memories of the autumn breeze caressing its leaves and the still of the moonlight on a winter night while that tree stood stoic in deep contemplation. And in the knowing of giving shelter in the spring and being a refuge to the song birds and the animals that called it home. Yes, while I witness the flickering of those flames, I see all of this and more, for the log in the fire is more than what it seems. It is at once an explosion of all its life's experiences and joys, and a reminder of what we leave behind, for this log has shown me, how even I, am connected to it all."

Enlightenment and awareness for the most part are one and the same, you cannot have enlightenment without having a heighten sense of awareness. Like in the quote above, there is a profound sense of inner-connectiveness through awareness that everything that is here is all part of something greater, that there is a Oneness, a one-mind and we are part of it. This is enlightenment.

The western world believes that with enlightenment, you attain some magical insight into the universe, that you receive some great dose of wisdom and knowledge. The truth is, enlightenment isn't about gaining. It is about losing. Enlightenment is the realization of the truth that there is nothing to find or attain. That truth becomes revealed in dropping all attachments, and all desires. In enlightenment, you see that there is nothing to know, that by losing it all, there is no need to attain anything. Enlightenment is the freedom from attachments and the need to be attached to anything or anybody.

-

CHAPTER NINE- WHAT IS THE TREE OF WISDOM AND WHO IS NAGARJUNA?

From the book, "Nagarjuna's Tree of Wisdom"

What is the Tree of Wisdom?

The Tree of Wisdom by Nagarjuna is a treatise on morals and ethics written over 2,000 years ago. This commentary on moral living is very similar to other text such as the Tao Te Ching by Lao Tzu, the Hsin Hsin Ming by Seng Ts'an, the Enchiridion by Epictetus, and Meditations by Marcus Aurelius.

It is remarkable that this is only the second English translation of this ancient text from this incredible Indian philosopher. The first translation into English was done by W.L. Campbell in 1918. At the time of Campbell's translation, there was so much already lost to history in the allegories that the meaning couldn't be extrapolated for all the verses.

This version has been interpreted into a more modern new age style yet it still possesses the essence of the message that Nagarjuna implied. I prefer to use the word interpretation over the word translation as this is more of a rendering constructed to clarify the meaning in such a way that it is easy to grasp the concepts. However, there are a few verses that have been left in the original Campbell translation as their relevance hasn't changed.

The primary difference between the Tree of Wisdom and the Tao Te Ching is the Tree of Wisdom takes a more "matter of fact" practical approach to life where the Tao Te Ching is more spiritual and esoteric. Both have the same basic underlying principles, they are just different paths to the same goal.

The Tree of Wisdom contains 260 verses containing just over 8,000 words. In the tradition of Buddhism, there are a few verses that will leave you confused. This is natural as in the contemplation of the verse, the understanding will become clear.

One major difference in this translation and Campbell's is the use of the way. Where the word "way" is used, it is to imply the way of the Tao Te Ching. I encourage those who are not familiar with the Tao Te Ching to read it as the two text complement each other.

To illustrate the concept of the Tree of Wisdom, here are a two of the verses within the text that convey the universal nature of the teachings of Nagarjuna. "Strive to have your accomplishments serve others, rather than have them serve your ego. If ego rules your actions, then how are morals attained?" and " Live life free of the fear of the unknown, for there is nothing to fear. Live life free of the fear of the known, for you can conquer those fears."

If all you did was just apply these two principles to your daily life, could you imagine the possibilities of the significant change that could take place in your life? Just overcoming your fears and living the life you truly desire and know that your actions are not only benefiting but others, wouldn't that be incredible? That would be change beyond measure. Now, just imagine if you applied more than just two verses to your life? Imagine immersing yourself into the wholeness of the text, what would your life be like? There is a whole new world waiting for you, all that is required is your willingness to get up and get going.

Who is Nagarjuna?

Nagarjuna was an Indian philosopher who lived around 150 to 250AD. He is credited with being the founder of the "Middle Path" (Madhyamaka) in the Buddhist school of the Mahayana Tradition. Nagarjuna is considered among scholars to be the most influential thinker after Gautama Buddha within Buddhism. As a matter of fact, Nagarjuna is considered to be the second Buddha among Tibetan and East Asian traditions of Buddhism.

There are several text and treatises attributed to Nagarjuna including the treatise on Rasayana Alchemy, and many sutras such as the 70 verses on

Emptiness, and Requisites of Enlightenment. Another important note is Nagarjuna is considered the one to have introduced the concept of "emptiness" to Buddhism. He also understood the dynamics of duality in that of existence and non-existence. He taught the concept of relativity in that our experiences are all comparative to our perception. There is only long because short exist, however what may be long to you might be short to someone else. He believed that one should strive for non-dualistic wisdom and compassion while living in a dualistic world. Within his teachings is the underlying message to live life in accordance with the laws of nature. Amazing that he was able to keep a common sense approach to his work that is easy to grasp. Even more amazing, his principles are strangely similar to the principles of Quantum Physics. This is remarkable considering that he lived about 1,800 years before the birth of Quantum Physics.

Like all Mystical Sages in Buddhism, little is known about the history of Nagarjuna. In the same tradition as Lao Tzu and Seng Ts'an, Nagarjuna's legend has become mythical. There are stories of Nagarjuna learning alchemy. It is said in legend that he used this lost art to transmute lead into gold to supply the Nalanda monks of the Nalanda Monastic University in northern India during a time of famine. There are several stories of Nagarjuna. One where he defeated 500 non-Buddhist in a debate.

Another story and perhaps the most fantastic is the

story of his death. It is said that the life span of Nagarjuna was attached to the King Udayibhadra. This king had a son, Kumara Shaktiman and he wanted to be the king. The king's wife, Kumara's mother, had instructed Kumara that in order to become king, he would need to cut Nagarjuna's head off. The mother also said that since Nagarjuna is such a compassionate man that surely he would agree.

Amazingly, Nagarjuna agreed however Kumara couldn't cut off his head with a sword. Nagarjuna said that in a previous life that he had killed an ant while cutting grass. Therefore, due to karma, only the blade of kusha grass could cut Nagarjuna. Kumara did this and was able to behead Nagarjuna. Strangely enough upon his supposed death, the blood coming from the severed head turned into milk and the head spoke, " Now, I will go to Sukhavati but I will enter this body once again." Sukhavati is the western pure land of the Buddha Amitabha. Sukhavati translates to mean, "Land of Bliss" Upon this revelation from the talking head, Kumara separated the head from the body as far as possible. However, legend states that every year the head and body become closer and closer to each other. When the head joins with the body, it is said that Nagarjuna will return to this world to walk again.

What is amazing about Nagarjuna besides the legends and writings, is while he is considered one of the most influential members of Buddhism, he is almost unknown outside the circles of Buddhism. I was shocked and surprised to see this text so obscure in today's world. I hope by bringing this ancient text to life again, the teachings of Nagarjuna will become as popular and well known as Lao Tzu's Tao Te Ching or Epictetus's Enchiridion.

CHAPTER TEN- THE IMPORTANCE OF THE TAO, A SHORT ESSAY

From the book- "The Importance of the Tao, A Short Essay"

"The mystery of life is not a problem to be solved, but a reality to be experienced"- Soren Kierkegaard

Why is the Tao important? The answer must be paradoxical in the sense that, "Those who know do not speak. Those who do speak do not know." So, as you can see, I'm somewhat in a predicament here with the subject. The paradoxical nature comes from trying to describe a singularity in a dualistic framework. As such, in order to comprehend the points being make, you first must bend your mind around the paradox until your mind becomes the paradox itself. When the unreal becomes more real than the real and the real begins to look unreal and you're utterly lost and confused, then friend, you're well on your way to getting "it." Welcome to the way of the Tao as you have taken your first step on the path of enlightenment and awareness. Smile as we celebrate you home!

We'll discuss three points in this essay. Truth, love, and the innerconnectiveness of life. The underlying principle in obtaining these points is through cultivating awareness. By cultivating awareness and striving to see the truth, the love, the innerconnectiveness of life, you'll find the path. In Eastern traditions, this way is called the Tao. In Mystic Christian traditions, it is the spiritual path to God. It doesn't matter what this path is called as it doesn't change the essence of its purpose.

Cultivating awareness is a form of spiritual development that leads to the divine source. Life within itself, if you will, is a spiritual journey. Awareness to this spiritual journey will allow you to make sense of life and stop being so tense. You'll understand the power of love and suffering. You'll learn how to ease the suffering and increase the love. You'll start living a life that is more purposeful and inspired. You'll find the bridge that crosses over from the dualism to the singularity. In realizing that we are all interconnected, your heart will overflow with unconditional love that is full of compassion. But most of all, to experience a love that for centuries, artist, poets, and musicians have been trying to convey into words. A love that is beyond words.

Truth-

"Truth is within ourselves; it takes no rise from outward things, whatever you may believe. There is an inmost center in us all, where truth abides in fullness."

Truth is a singularity. With the singularity being the divine source. There is only one truth as within the singularity, there is only one. However, we live in a dualist world. With duality we must have an up for a down, a left for a right, a right must need a wrong. In a dualist world, one cannot exist unless there is an opposite. Everything must have an opposite, that's the rule of dualism. There must be two.

Since truth is a singularity, any truth brought into this world is a variation, a version of the one truth. As such, even though it contains some essence of the one truth, it is still diluted. It is to be questioned and doubted. Even this truth should be scrutinized. Any truth translated from the divine source into this world and into a language cannot be pure.

The only way a person can come to see and experience this one pure truth, this singular truth, is from within himself. While we live in a dualist world, our essence, our soul, our true self, are born of the singularity, of the divine. This is where we are all from and where we will all return to one day. We are so much more than our thoughts and our actions in this life. We are more than this life. All this life is, is just another pearl on a endless strand. But we have become so caught up living in this illusion that we have forgotten who we really are and where we came from. In that forgetfulness, we have lost sight of the one pure truth that we have within ourselves.

Imagine for a moment that your life is part of a play, a grand theatrical production and you're the star. In this play you are playing the leading role, the main character. And like any good theatrical production, the storyline contains trials and tribulations, heroes and villains, and a supporting cast of other stars. After this production runs its course and comes to an end, all the actors, stage hands, and support staff will take a break before embarking on another play.

This is the way life is, just another play. However, it went wrong when you, the actor, forgot that you are the actor. Instead you have come to believe that this character you're playing is really you, the real you. And as such, you have developed some fears along the way, the biggest fear being that when the play ends, you'll end with it too. This is what we refer to as death. Because we are so wrapped up in this illusion, we cannot see the truth as we have forgotten about it. We are so deeply implanted into a belief system that it makes change nearly impossible. We cling to the only thing we know, and that is this character we are playing at the moment, and the belief that this fantasy is a reality.

The first step to finding the truth is to break free from this belief system. You must awaken from this dream and realize that all of this that you are experiencing is real. When you are able to wake up and see the truth, you'll see that not only are you just playing a part in a play, you'll also see that you have the power to rewrite your part, to take control of it and make it your own. That you can become the director and create whatever it is that you desire. More importantly, you will see that you are more than just this one life, more than whatever you have done or will do in this life. You will know that you are an eternal soul belonging to eternity and all of this is only a drop in an endless ocean.

In going about discovering the one truth, it isn't about trying to go out and look for it, it is more about removing what you think is real and what you have been clinging to. It is in casting off old belief systems and ridding yourself of the thoughts of the ego. It is in taking these steps that will allow the one pure truth to shine through. The one truth has always been here and always will be. With this revelation, you will see that you are indeed a singularity at your core masked by the confines of a dualistic world. The one pure truth resides within your soul; it is part of you and your essence.

This is the paradoxical nature of a singularity within a dualist world. Yes, a singularity can exist in a dualistic world. We are living proof of that fact. A great illustration of this phenomenon can be found in a magnet. Take a magnet; it has a north and south pole. No matter how many times you cut a magnet in half, there will always be a north and south pole. This is the laws of physics at work. There must always be a north and south pole. Even if you could cut the magnet down to the smallest size known to man, there would still be this dualism within the magnet.

However, there in that magnet is a place at the center where there is no north or south pole, no dualism, only a singularity. You can't see it, and science can't find it either, but it does exist. It is there. The primary reason we cannot see it is because we are looking at it through the eyes of dualism. The first law of dualism is you must have the exact opposite of any one thing for the thing to exist. This is the key that has eluded man from the beginning. We are trying to look for something that cannot be seen from the perspective of dualism. Just because you cannot see it doesn't mean that it doesn't exit. Whatever you choose to believe or not to believe doesn't change the truth. Just as you cannot show me your soul, yet you know you have one, it is the same with the one truth.

The one truth is within you and you are the only one who can rediscover it. Within you is the answer to every question but you are the only one who can unlock that door. All I, or for that matter anyone can do, is to show the shadows of the one truth, the hints, suggestions, implications of this truth, but never the full truth itself, for the one pure truth can only be experienced from within yourself.

An example of living this truth is in the song "Walt Grace's Submarine Test, January 1967" by John Mayer. It shows that following your heart is more important then what people say or think. That when you're done with this world, the next one is up to you.

"Walt Grace, desperately hating his old place
Dreamed to discover a new space and buried himself alive
Inside his basement
The tongue on the side of his face meant
He's working away on displacement
And what it would take to survive

'Cause when you're done with this world
You know the next is up to you

And his wife told his kids he was crazy
And his friends said he'd fail if he tried
But with the will to work hard and a library card
He took a homemade, fan blade, one-man submarine ride

That morning the sea was mad and I mean it
Waves as big as he'd seen it deep in his dreams at home
From dry land, he rolled it over to wet sand
Closed the hatch up with one hand
And pedaled off alone

'Cause when you're done with this world
You know the next is up to you

And for once in his life, it was quiet
As he learned how to turn in the tide
And the sky was aflare when he came up for air
In his homemade, fan blade, one-man submarine ride

One evening, when weeks had passed since his leaving
The call she planned on receiving finally made it home
She accepted the news she never expected
The operator connected the call from Tokyo
'Cause when you're done with this world
You know the next is up to you

Now his friends bring him up when they're drinking
At the bar with his name on the side
And they smile when they can, as they speak of the man
Who took a homemade, fan blade, one-man submarine ride"

Whatever truth was meant for Walt Grace, he was able to discover and follow it. Even though it caused friction with his friends and family, he never lost sight of his goal and stay on the path. He was able to see the bigger picture and trust in himself and follow his truth.

So this truth, where is it and how do you get to it? Ah, I cannot give you the answer, however, I can give you some thoughts to contemplate in helping you search for it. First off, start living with a conviction of the heart. Stop living in your mind and start living in your heart. Stop living the life that is meant of you by others. Live life independently of the good opinions of others. The most important responsibility is not to the nation you live in, or to the church you go to, or to anyone other than yourself. The most important responsibility is to yourself. Get out of your ego and into your heart. Stop listening to other people and start listening to your heart.

When I say heart, I am talking about that intuitive part of you. That inner voice that has been speaking to you since your earliest days. Learn to trust in yourself and in that voice. That voice is the authentic part of you that is from the singularity, from the divine source. It would bid you well to listen as it will never steer you wrong. Even when everything in your mind is saying no, have faith in yourself and follow your heart. This voice, this intuitive part of you is the bridge that will allow you to cross back to the divine source, back to the singularity.

Learn to tell the difference between your authentic self and your ego. Now how do I know the difference? Another great question that I can answer. When you are motivated to take action, is it because it is the right thing to do or is it to bring you recognition, glory, or self-gratification? Are your motives based on unconditional love or compassion or are they based in getting ahead in the rat race? One point to remember about the rat race is that even if you win it, you're still a rat. Why be in a race where there is no clear starting or finishing line? And just who are you racing against? Opt out of this meaningless race so you may find what it is that you seek.

Let me give you an example of taking action and knowing the difference between the authentic self and the ego. While I was working on the Indigo book, I would often stop in at the local convenience store when a break was needed. The clerk was from Nepal and we would have some meaty discussions on eastern thought. He once asked what I did and I replied that I was a writer. Well, he laughed and assumed I was just another one of the unemployed folks in the neighborhood that hung out with nothing to do other than seek for self-importance. To be honest, yes, it did bother me a little, not being taken seriously. Therefore, when the book came out, I took him a copy, for no other reason than to show him that I was indeed an author. Yes, he was surprised to say the least. This little tale illustrates how this act did nothing but feed my ego and yes it served to create self-importance. It was about showing him who I was, that I was somebody. If I had been living in my authentic self, this wouldn't have been necessary. This was nothing more an act to feed my ego. This is living in the world with the belief that you are part of the world.

A few months later, I was in a home improvement store and needed some help in finding a particular item. I had an older gentleman that worked there assist me. During our time together, he shared his story about getting his life back on track. He had been homeless and had some really tough issues to overcome. However, he was able to turn his life around. He said the biggest lesson he learn from his darkest days was that it wasn't always about him. He had created a life that was all about him and how he blamed everyone for his misfortune, forgetting that we are all brothers and sisters. When he was able to wake up to the truth he took responsibility for his actions. He saw that life is about helping each other and we how we treat each other. It is about the love you have and share. It's about the choices we make. He said that he now strives to not be so selfish or self-centered, and instead looks for opportunities to help others. He discovered that the key to receiving what it is that you want is to first give it away. In helping others, he is helping himself.

I was moved by this man's story and his desire to regain his life. After I checked out and went to the car, I grabbed a copy of one of my books and went back inside to give it to him. All I said was thank you for the assistance and that here was a book for him that might be helpful. I didn't tell him who I was or that I was the one that wrote the book. It was simply a gesture to help someone who was trying to find his way. That was what this act was about. This act came from my authentic self, no ego, no self-glorification, no need for importance, just an act of compassion in helping a brother.

I hope these two illustrations help in showing the difference between acting out of ego versus acting out of the authentic self. One point to keep in mind is that we are all human and will continue to commit acts to feed our ego; that cannot be avoided. However, by cultivating awareness, we can become aware when we are about to feed the ego and take the necessary steps to correct the actions if necessary.

Now the paradox of this is sometimes we must feed the ego. As much as the ego is an obstruction to spiritual growth, it can serve as a survival mechanism from time to time. However, do not get caught up in it too deeply. Finding balance and control between your ego and authentic self is an art - an art that requires constant practice.

Some last thoughts on truth. Live in the now, in the moment, in the present. Do not let tomorrow be the answer to yesterday's dreams. When you do, you are living life in between and not in the moment. The sorrow that your conscience will bring to you will be created by your ego. The wisdom you think you know because of these actions is not wisdom. Rather it is a justification of your actions disguised as wisdom. Learn to live your dreams today, even if only in your mind.

Learn to pay attention. Practice awareness. Make it a point to become more aware of everything, especially your thoughts. Become aware of how you react to different things as they happen in your life. By doing this, you'll soon see how your thinking affects your reality. By shifting your focus inward and stripping away the old thought patterns and beliefs, you'll begin to see the path to the truth. Abraham Maslow said, - "What is necessary to change a person is to change his awareness of himself." Everything you need is already within yourself. You have the power, the power to create the change you desire. The power is within and within that power, you'll find the truth.

Love-

"Now is the moment to dive as deep as your dream. Love is the greatest freedom when you love a courageous person. It allows for an entirely different experience of life than the freedom of journeying alone. Wherever you are, you know you are loved, not only by God, but by a mirror of yourself." - Kenny Loggins

Everyone at one time or another has felt a love that transcends words. There has been moments when we have experienced a bliss that is beyond this world. This is a love that we would all want to experience all the time. There are different types of love but the love we are going to address in this essay is the divine love. Divine love transcends life and death, and lives on forever and ever. It is an energy that has radiated throughout the universe since before the dawn of time. The incredible aspect of this love is anyone can experience it right now. There are no mountains to climb, no oceans to sail, and no crosses to bear. It is here right now, always has been and always will be. All that it takes is awareness. Through cultivating awareness, you can unlock the door to a love that is beyond this world. The paradox to this is you have the key to the door. The door is locked from inside and you don't even realize that you are sitting there in the dark, all along holding the key.

Like finding truth, it isn't about going out and looking for it. Rather it is about stripping away a lifetime of false beliefs and clinging to a system that has been preventing you from discovering that all you ever really wanted and needed was already in your possession.

Now the paradoxical nature of this divine love is found in equanimity. To give an illustration of this principle can be seen in the definition of freedom. Only those who have lost their freedom truly know the meaning and value of it. How can you cherish a concept like freedom if you have always had it? With nothing to compare it to, how would you know the difference? This is the dilemma - how can you value something if you have no clue of its value? This is true with love; you'll never know the real meaning and value of love until you have lost a love like this. Ah, yes, the curse of living in a dualistic world; you can't have one without the other. This is where equanimity comes into play.

Equanimity can be found in the Tao. Verse 13 shows this principle, " Meet failure or success with grace, honor and kindness. Accept misfortune or fortune with grace, honor and kindness. Why? Do not be concerned with either. Accept all that comes your way. Good and evil comes from having a body, which is the cost of being human. Good or evil cannot affect the true essence of the soul. The soul of man is everlasting. Surrender yourself and love all that comes your way. See yourself in all that comes your way. See the divine perfection in the Mother of the universe. Know that you are one with all. In doing so you will be trusted to care for all things"

Equanimity is the highest state of consciousness, the highest state of unconditional love. It is a conditioning of the mind, a form of enlightenment. Equanimity is a lesson in being detached but not removed from the experiences of life. Equanimity is learning to be responsible for yourself as well as others by knowing that you have the power to stop the pain and suffering. Knowing that you have this power to bring an end to pain and suffering and replace it with unconditional love, compassion, and kindness will keep you in a tranquil state of peace.

In the world of Christian Mystics, this principle is known as being Christ-like. Equanimity is a quality that Christ mastered and demonstrated throughout his life. Like attracts like. It is what you project out onto this world that will reflect within yourself. In the study of the great mystics, this is the one common thread. In order to meet Christ face to face, you must become like Christ. And it doesn't have to be Christ, it can be any great avatar that has walked on this earth. Equanimity is the path that must be traveled in order to arrive at the destination you desire in finding divine love.

Equanimity doesn't require constant thought, but it does require being in a state of awareness of being in the now and the knowing that all living beings are connected. By learning forgiveness and selflessness, you'll see that whatever you give to others, you are giving back to yourself.

Part of this comes from being the observer. In being an observer, there is a degree of detachment from the constraints of the illusionary world. This is a freedom, knowing that you are more than what you appear to be, more than just a human having a human experience. That you are a spiritual being having a human experience, like an actor playing a part in a play.

Equanimity can be compared to a mirror. Imagine a mirror that reflects reality, it reflects the images without judgment or prejudice. The mirror simply reflects whatever is cast across its surface. The mirror doesn't ask for the images nor does it reject them. It accepts whatever comes across its surface, as this is the purpose of a mirror. It doesn't try to hold on to any of the images or try to identify with the images. It just reflects the world as it is presented to it. The principles of equanimity and divine love are like this.

Detachment within equanimity, like a mirror is illustrated in verse 16 of the Tao, "Empty yourself completely. Bring your mind to rest and your heart to peace. Allow the ten thousand things to come and go while just observing. See how one ending is just another beginning. See the serenity in the movement to and fro from the divine source. Come to know the eternal wisdom by returning to the divine source and realize your destiny. For this is the enlightenment of the Tao. Knowing that all is everlasting. Even after the death of the body, you will remain whole in the Tao"

Most people need to identify with events and experiences in order to have a sense of who they are; this is the ego at work. This is the roadblock that holds most people back from learning equanimity. Within a state of equanimity, you are not identified by any of these. One must temper their ego first before taking on the art of equanimity. The purpose of the ego is to acquire and to attach to whatever it can, including people, while with equanimity - it is about being detached from these things. Like in the Tao, don't grow attached to anything that will bring sorrow if removed.

In equanimity, you'll respond with the same unconditional loving kindness and compassion to whatever experiences come your way. The tricky part to this is you will still feel pain and suffering as well as love and joy. This is a necessary part of being human, feeling emotions. The difference is with equanimity, you'll treat all experiences the same. You will not react in a vengeful manner or repay a negative compliment with a negative response.

Instead, you will study the experience, play with it, ask why, look at it inside and out, learn from it and then let it go. It is creating a state of evenness that is unbiased to the events and people involved. Just an understanding that it is what it is, nothing more. Equanimity serves to teach that within a dualistic framework, pain and suffering is necessary in order to experience true love and joy.

To whatever level of pain you experience, you'll be able to experience love on the same level. You cannot know ecstatic levels of joy and pain with knowing the abysmal depths of pain. This is the grace that heals, knowing that in the darkness of painful events, you can rejoice with sympathetic joy and respond with unconditional love and compassion while staying in a tranquil state of peace.

There is a song by the pop group Bread called, "It Don't Matter to Me" written by Davis Gates that illustrates this principle of loving without attachment while still being compassionate, a knowing of how we are connected. To some the lyrics may seem cold hearted and distant, but those with an awareness of the Tao will see the true meaning in the words. A beautiful song that clearly represents unconditional love and compassion while staying centered in peace,

"It don't matter to me
If you really feel that

You need some time to be free
Time to go out searching for yourself
Hoping to find
Time ... to go to find

It don't matter to me
If you take up with
Someone who's better than me
'Cause your happiness is all I want
For you to find
Peace ... your peace of mind

A lot of people have an ego hang-up
'Cause they want to be the only one
How many came before it really doesn't matter
Just as long as you're the last
Everybody's moving on and try to find out
What's been missing in the past

And it don't matter to me
If your searching brings you back together with me
'Cause there'll always be
An empty room waiting for you
An open heart waiting for you
Time is on my side ...

'Cause it don't matter to me ...
'Cause there'll always be
An empty room waiting for you
An open heart waiting for you
Time is on my side ...

We are all from the same divine source, all part of the same divine creation; we all have a divine perfection within each and every one of us. Even when other people don't see this perfection, you will. You'll see the many masks of God in everyone you meet.

This is the essence of divine love that you need to understand. This isn't a pick and choose situation, even though you think it is. There must be an "all accepting, all encompassing" nature that comes from the knowing that we are part of the same. Life is not always a walk in the park, at times it will be nightmarish and seemly unbearable. With life, you take it all, the good with the bad. You treat it all the same from the standpoint of love.

Like Bruce Springsteen said in the song "Tunnel of Love,"

"It ought to be easy ought to be simple enough Man meets woman and they fall in love But the house is haunted and the ride gets rough And you've got to learn to live with what you can't rise above if you want to ride on down in through this tunnel of love"

You have to learn to take the bad with the good. Maybe the bad is there because you need to learn from it or maybe it is a reflection of something in you. The point being, all of this is by divine design and everything has a purpose and reason. In seeking this divine love, you must drop the ego self along with the rulebook.

What does this divine love look like? How do you know it? This love I am talking about is the love you find and how you share it with others. It's about how you're going to spend your time with your lover, about the give and take, and how you treat each other. It's all about the friends you make. It's all about your choices. It's on the importance of forgiving and being forgiven. To live a life that is pure in faith and heart. To strive to stay on the path of love. To find the way of the masters that have gone before us. To recognize the path that they forge for us and the wisdom to see it. It is in not trying to posses someone, it is allowing them to be who it is that they are meant to be. This is a love that connects at the soul level, that level that transcends life and death, a love that transcends any boundary know to man. It is a true, pure, and honest love. You will know this love when it comes to you; it will nest in your heart and will remain there as long as you are true to it. You'll just know it when you feel it, you will know.

You biggest enemy in attaining this love is your ego. Don't allow your ego to destroy this love. It will try to create separation and will want to become possessive. Jealously and envy are born in the ego. The ego has a hang up about being the only one and living in the past. Your true authentic self doesn't know anything about jealously or envy. Your authentic self doesn't care about how many have come before you met your soul mate, all that matters is you found one another. Learn to tell when your ego is trying to take control and keep a vigil on your love, as it will last well past this life into the next one. Do not allow anything or anyone to come between you and your right as a spiritual being to true love. Guard it like a king that treasures his gold.

When you find that someone special, that true love, your soul mate, know that you have found the other half of yourself. Stay true and love will show you the way, love is the answer, love is the key, love is the light.

Knowing and experiencing true love is the essence of life. Knowing and experiencing the divine love is the quest of life. Not knowing these is living a living death. Choose Life! Choose Love!

Innerconnectiveness of Life-

"All my life has been a struggle in trying to get free. But this world I created turned out to be only about me. Forgetting we are brothers" - Kenny Loggins

"All of our lives we have pretended and hidden our feelings from others. We have tried hard to believe that there is this distance between us. In this misperception, we thought we could find comfort in isolation. However, this comfort is fleeting when the soul speaks up in a longing for something more meaningful. It's about how to stop pretending and start being true to yourself. It's about stopping making excuses and taking responsibility for your actions.

All of our life has been a struggle in trying to be free but the reality is the life you have created has been all about you. This is because you have allowed your ego to rule over you. In this realization comes a sense of freedom, a release from your self-imposed prison. When you have the key, you can unlock the doors of this dungeon and step into the light of the divine love of the way. Once in the light, you'll see that we all are brothers and sisters, all part of something bigger than we can imagine. In this oneness, there is a liberation of knowing that life and death are only illusions."

This is the biggest illusion next to the concept of death. The illusion is kept alive by the belief that we are all separated from one another. There is no separation between any of us or with nature. All this so-called separation is nothing more than a creation of the collective ego of humankind. It is this separation that gives the ego power over us, and not just us as individuals but separation allows for just a few to rule over the masses. Just this one aspect of the ego is responsible for more death, destruction, and misery than any other thing that man has created. With this concept of separation, there have been wars since the dawn of man. How many have died in the name of this or that religion? How many have died because their blood was different? How many have died because of their skin color? Slavery was born out of the concept of separation. How else could a civilized man agree to imprison another man, unless he felt, no, knew in his mind that this other person wasn't a human like him? Separation has been the most destructive force on the planet. Moreover, it doesn't stop with man verses man, it has extended to killing off fish and animals. With the buffalo, the whales, with several fish and birds, how many species have become extinct in the name of progress because of being disconnected?

This is the one evil concept that man has created that still is in practice today and will be until the end of times. This is the one mistake that continues to happen over and over every generation. How many more will die under the flag of separation and how many more species will only be kept alive through history books, all in the name of progress?

The Native Americans knew this principle of innerconnectiveness better than most. One only needs to look at the beliefs of the Native Americans to see the evidence of their profound respect of nature. The Native Americans would only kill animals for food or in defense, and never for sport. They would never cut down a living tree for firewood unless there were no other options. They had respect for all living things because they knew the innerconnectiveness of the universal consciousness.

They considered themselves caretakers of their domain. They never saw themselves as owners with the right to do whatever they felt like doing. They maintained their respect for nature, which was first and foremost in their lives. They considered themselves responsible for how they left the land for at least the next seven generations. In the Western world, I doubt most people even think about how what they are doing will make an impact next year much, less what kind of legacy we are leaving for our grandchildren's grandchildren.

The Native Americans had an understanding of the innerconnectiveness of life and nature. It is engrained into their belief system. For a group of people with no organized structure or resemblance to the Western world, they seem to had a deep profound knowledge of the mysteries of life.

They lived in peace and harmony not only with their fellow man but also with nature. Black Elk is quoted for saying this about peace, "The first peace, which is the most important, is that which comes within the souls of people when they realize their relationship, their oneness with the universe and all its powers, and when they realize that at the center of the universe dwells the Great Spirit, and that this center is really everywhere, it is within each of us."

The Tao covers this thought in verse 14, " What cannot be seen is invisible. What cannot be heard is inaudible. That which cannot be held is intangible. These three are beyond definition. Therefore they are as one. With no form or sound, they cannot be described. As they are from the nothingness that is unseen, unheard and untouchable. There is no light at rising. There is no darkness at setting. It continues in a place where there is no time or space. Embrace it and you'll find no beginning or end. You cannot know it but you can be part of it. Embrace the experience beyond words and feel the essence of the Tao."

Following is a passage from the book Hsin Hsin Ming. It is on the innerconnectiveness of nature and how we are all part of the one. It offers a very interesting perspective on this principle. "Upon returning home on a cold winter night, I begin my evening by building a fire in the fireplace to chase away the chill. Once I have gather the logs and placed them so, I start the fire. At the birth of the flames starting to flicker among the logs, it is in that moment I know that I am releasing all the memories that have been stored up in that tree. I know that I am releasing the sunshine that gave warmth to that tree , that tree from whence the firewood came. I know that I am releasing the clouds that gave it shade, the rain that quench its thirst, the soil from which it received its nourishment, and all those enjoyments that the tree experienced so joyfully, like those memories of the autumn breeze caressing its leaves and the still of the moonlight on a winter night while that tree stood stoic in deep contemplation. And in the knowing of giving shelter in the spring and being a refuge to the song birds and the animals that called it home. Yes, while I witness the flickering of those flames, I see all of this and more, for the log in the fire is more than what it seems. It is at once an explosion of all its life's experiences and joys, and a reminder of what we leave behind, for this log has shown me, how even I, am connected to it all."

Once awakened to the truth that everything on this planet is connected, you'll feel a sense of hurt, shame, but most of all, an anger will build inside of you at all the atrocities being committed. Then you'll understand the value of the truth and love and it how plays into the way you'll think. Even with all this death and destruction, you'll find equanimity. With this you'll draw your strength as it will be the divine love that gives you courage and truth that will guide you.

When you have this revelation, you'll see everyone and everything in a different light. You'll have a deep compassion and feel a connection to every living thing. There will be a sense of just knowing that even a piece of firewood burning in the fireplace contains a connection to you. You'll see the clouds, the sunlight, and the rain in the paper that has been used to print this book. You'll be able to feel the love of nature and see the harmonic balance of life when left to its own accord.

You'll be hard pressed to bring any harm on anything, even that pesky cricket that is driving you nuts in the living room. Rather than ending his life with the Sunday Times, you'll catch him and return him to his place in nature. When the people around you joke about it, you'll just smile, knowing secretly that you know a love, a truth, a sense of belonging that they will never know. You'll understand what Kenny Loggins was singing in I'm Alright," I'm alright, nobody worry about me. Why you got to give me a fight? Can't you just let it be? I'm alright, I'm alright, just let me be."

You'll feel alive and ten feet tall as you see the world as it is and what your part is within it. You'll find more solace walking in the park among the trees and the songbirds than you will sitting at a bar during happy hour. Your transformation will be profound indeed, and no one around you will ever know the difference, and that will be fine with you. This dilemma has been around forever, even Plato said, "Those who are able to see beyond the shadows and lies of their culture will never be understood, yet alone believed, by the masses."

With this new found freedom, you'll love a little more, you'll hold your loved ones a little tighter, a little longer, you'll say "I love you" a little more often. You'll go a little slower as to not miss a beautiful sunset, to listen to the song of a bird, to marvel at the wonderment of the leaves on a tree dancing in the breeze on your way home.

If not already, you'll begin to start treating animals with a new respect. Like Arthur Schopenhauer said, "Compassion for animals is intimately connected to the goodness of character; and it may be confidently asserted that he who is cruel to animals cannot be a good man." It will be as if you are able to empathically communicate with animals. You'll just know what they are thinking. If you have a dog or a cat, you'll notice a deeper level to the relationship that you won't be able to explain. You'll no longer have a burning desire to hunt or fish for sport.

More importantly will be your relationship with your lover. Combined with the truth, the love and the knowing of being connected, your love will transcend life and death. You'll have a love that most people will never experience, never know that it even exists. You will rediscover each other again and marvel at how you found each other in this life. You will have a love so strong that nothing on this earth can break it. It is a feeling of being complete and whole.

When you hear a love song written from the heart, you will be able to truly hear it and know exactly what is being sung. You'll get goose bumps in the knowing that a true love is being sung about, and you will feel more alive than ever before. You will be living in the way.

"Whenever I call you friend, I begin to think I understand. Anywhere we are, you and I have always been, ever and ever. I see myself in your eyes, and that's all I need to show me why. Everything I do always takes me home to you, ever and ever. Now I know that life had given me more than memories, day by day, we can see in every moment there's a reason to carry on. Sweet Love is showing us a heavenly light, never seen such a beautiful sight. See love glowing on us every night. I know forever we'll be doing it right. You're the glowing light in my life, source of pride in my life. Everything I do takes me back to you." - Kenny Loggins

ABOUT THE AUTHOR

Dennis Waller, author of several books including the #1 Best Seller on Amazon Kindle, "Tao Te Ching, A Translation,", is recognized as an expert on spiritual experience, self-discovery, and exploring the human consciousness. As writer, speaker and philosopher, his teachings invoke an introspective view on how to discover one's true authentic self through a higher sense of consciousness and awareness. He teaches classes in the Dallas area on several subjects including Enochian Magic and Developing Your Psychic Abilities. He is best known for his work in the field of Indigos, people who possess unusual or supernatural abilities. His other fields of expertise include comparative religion, the law of attraction, and interpreting Eastern thought's relevancy to science and quantum physics. He is in demand as a guest speaker on radio programs, a lecturer at churches and life enrichment groups, and conducts workshops for Indigos.

He doesn't like long walks on the beach at night unless it is with the love of his life nor does he care for round colorful balloons but he does enjoy an occasional game of cricket on a sunny spring day. This bit of non-sense is included to see if you really read these bios. If you have then you will enjoy his sense of humor. Never take life too seriously, you will die someday so make the most of it, go out for an ice-cream, feed the ducks and tell someone you love that you do love them, even if they're mad at you, unless they're really really mad like someone I know, (hint hint), then, just maybe a phone call would be better.

Now, enough with the non-sense, but really, find a way to enjoy live and love!

Feel free to contact the author
@ dennismwaller@yahoo.com

Other Books by Dennis Waller

Zen and Tao, A Little Book on Buddhist Thought

Hsin Hsin Ming

Are You an Indigo? Discover Your Authentic Self

The Art of Talking to Christ

The Tao of Kenny Loggins

Indigo Wisdom with Francesca Rivera

Tao Te Ching- A Translation

Nagarjuna's Tree of Wisdom

Please go to
www.amazon.com/DennisWaller/e/B009HBKD8M
for a complete list of books & audio books

notes

DENNIS WALLER

notes

notes

notes